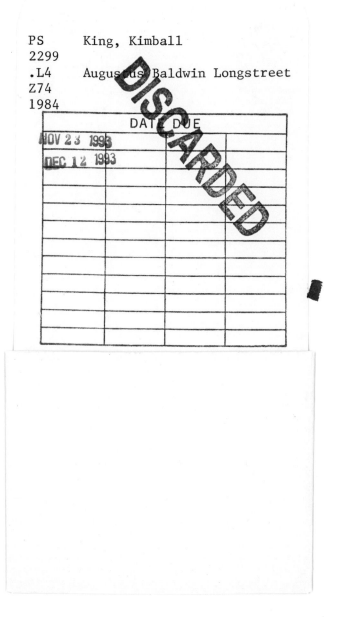

Augustus Baldwin Longstreet

Twayne's United States Authors Series

TUSAS 474

AUGUSTUS BALDWIN LONGSTREET
(1790–1870)
*Photograph courtesy of Special Collection,
Robert W. Woodruff Library, Emory University*

Augustus Baldwin Longstreet

By Kimball King

University of North Carolina at Chapel Hill

Twayne Publishers • Boston

Augustus Baldwin Longstreet

Kimball King

Copyright © 1984 by G. K. Hall & Company
All Rights Reserved
Published by Twayne Publishers
A Division of G. K. Hall & Company
70 Lincoln Street
Boston, Massachusetts 02111

Book Production by Marne B. Sultz

Book Design by Barbara Anderson

Printed on permanent/durable acid-free
paper and bound in the United States of
America.

**Library of Congress Cataloging in
Publication Data.**

King, Kimball.
  Augustus Baldwin Longstreet.

  (Twayne's United States authors series; TUSAS 474)
  Bibliography: p. 146
  Includes index.
  1. Longstreet, Augustus Baldwin, 1790–1870—
Criticism and interpretation.
  I. Title   II. Series.
PS2299.L4Z74   1984   813'.3   84–6652
ISBN 0–8057–7415–7

To Mrs. B. H. with love and wonder

Contents

About the Author

Kimball King was born in Princeton, New Jersey, on February 5, 1934. He graduated from the Lawrenceville School and attended Yale and Johns Hopkins universities. On December 27, 1955, he was married to Harriet Richards Lowry of Washington, D. C. The Kings have three children.

After four years of preparatory school teaching in Connecticut, King returned to graduate school at the University of Wisconsin where he received his Ph.D. in 1964. That year he joined the English faculty at the University of North Carolina at Chapel Hill, where he teaches courses in American literature and in contemporary British and American drama. From 1966 to 1976, he served as bibliographer for the American Literature Section of the Modern Language Association. During those same years, he was a regional chairman of *American Literary Manuscripts,* which was published in 1977. King has contributed articles and reviews to the *Mississippi Quarterly,* the *Southern Humanities Review, Modern Drama, Genre,* and other periodicals and collections of essays. His critical edition of Thomas Nelson Page's *In Ole Virginia* appeared in 1969 and was followed by *Twenty Modern British Playwrights* (1977), *Ten Modern Irish Playwrights* (1979), and *Ten Modern American Playwrights* (1982). Presently he is the managing editor of the *Southern Literary Journal.*

Preface

The literary reputation of Augustus Baldwin Longstreet rests primarily on *Georgia Scenes,* a collection of sketches published first in 1835, concerning life in middle Georgia in the early nineteenth century. His "scenes" were drawn from his experiences as a circuit judge and, in their concentration on rural poor whites, provide the first significant alternative to the plantation tradition in southern literature. Longstreet was bright, energetic, and ambitious, and he held unshakeable moral convictions. Wishing to be famous above all else, he particularly hoped to be identified as a kind of social philosopher—someone who would guide others in the creation of a perfect democratic community. He dreamed of an essentially agrarian society, led by an educated, benevolent few who would be dedicated to hard work and religious affirmation.

Five years after the publication of his famous work, Longstreet became president of Emory College, then in Oxford, Georgia. In his inaugural address, he outlined his hopes for the youth of Georgia and the role they would play in shaping southern life, its institutions, and values:

A race of better spirits has risen up, who perceive that all that is dear to the Christian, the philanthropist, the patriot and the statesman, is involved in the moral and intellectual improvement of the people. Accordingly we see them from their own resources erecting schools and colleges in all quarters of the state, and, what is equally gratifying, we see some of the most promising young men of the state, and the sons of some of the most distinguished men of the state, taking places in these institutions as preceptors. I rejoice with joy unspeakable at this state of things. I rejoice that the gifted sons of the soil begin to discover that there are other and more useful fields of labor for talent at this time, than the forum or senate house. I rejoice that I have lived to see the dawn, or rather the return of that patriotism which looks to the permanent good of the country.

Here the new president reveals the central theme of every story or essay he ever wrote: the need to remain in harmony with nature, to till the soil, to cherish one's roots in the simple pioneer past while assimilating the lasting benefits of civilization—education, religion, government.

Longstreet became a celebrity in the antebellum South. Four times a college president, he combined moral and religious fervor with the reasoning of a barrister and engaged actively in preparing his students for life in the South as he saw it. He was a staunch states' rights conservative, and although he bitterly opposed the war, his public denunciations of northern opposition to slavery contributed to the sectional hostility that preceded it. As an educator he influenced several generations of southern leaders—among them his nephew, James Longstreet, Robert E. Lee's friend and a general in the Civil War, and his son-in-law, L. Q. C. Lamar, who became the leading southern statesman after the war. In *Georgia Scenes* he created the first literary impression of the early life of his state and—what was probably a clearer and more important contribution from his own vantage point—in his public and private life he stood as a model of the dignified, hard-working, dependable patriarch for generations of young southerners and for his own devoted family.

Chapter One of this book is primarily biographical and discusses Longstreet's five separate careers as lawyer-judge, politician, clergyman, educator, and author. His first biographer, Bishop Oscar P. Fitzgerald, writing two decades after the author's death, had personal contact with old Georgians, surviving friends, and relatives. Fitzgerald's scholarship in *Judge Longstreet* (1891) provides nearly all the substantive personal information that is available because Longstreet's own records were destroyed by fire in his granddaughter's home; but his unqualified admiration for the Judge frequently resulted in biased or oversimplified interpretations of the latter's life and works. In 1924 John Donald Wade, in *Augustus Baldwin Longstreet: A Study of the Developments of Culture in the South,* widened the scope of Fitzgerald's biography by providing a more balanced and complex analysis of Longstreet's written works. Wade's style is charming but discursive, presenting the author's life in anecdotes that are seldom sequential. The present study is the first to place the major events of the author's life in a chronological order, and it attempts to capture his compelling, often contradictory, personality.

In the second chapter, *Georgia Scenes* is subjected to intensive literary analysis. Each scene is discussed separately in terms of its subject matter and its history of prior publication, if any. Then the organization of the entire collection in one book is described so that its dominant themes can be identified. In particular, the roles of the separate narrators of *Georgia Scenes* are discussed, since each seems to be a spokesman for a particular view of southern life. Until recently, *Georgia Scenes* has been valued primarily for providing an alternative to the plantation literary tradition and for introducing a new source of native materials—middle Georgia with its pioneers and poor whites. Scholars have often overlooked Longstreet's description of an emerging class of business men, entrepreneurs and social climbers, who were to become social and political leaders during the author's lifetime.

Chapter Three begins with a detailed review of the critical reception accorded Longstreet's major work from his own time until the present day. It attempts as well to point out the extent of his literary influence. Finally it discusses his minor writings in the years immediately following the publication of the *Scenes,* such as his stories for the *Magnolia,* his letters on the *Epistle of Paul to Philemon,* and *The Voice from the South.* In the next chapter, Longstreet's experiences as a college president are further scrutinized, along with his educational and social theories. A close reading of the critically neglected novel, *Master William Mitten; or, A Youth of Brilliant Talents Who Was Ruined by Bad Luck,* uncovers a perceptive psychological and environmental study, which offers insights into the emotions of a troubled boy as well as satirical glimpses of a community hardening into value systems abhorrent to the author. This chapter also discusses the author's reaction to his novel's lack of popularity and his preoccupation with volatile religious and political issues in the years preceding the Civil War, his experiences during the war, and his final efforts, in literature and in life, to assert his Jeffersonian ideals in an increasingly pluralistic society. The final chapter examines Longstreet as a precursor of the local color movement and evaluates the significance of three new editions of *Georgia Scenes* issued during that literary era, as well as the appearance in 1912 of *Stories with a Moral,* a collection of previously published writings.

Throughout the text, the author's major literary contributions are emphasized: his special use of the southern oral storytelling tradition, his dependence on the neglected Piedmont region for new sources of southern literary experience, his attempt to identify conflicting cultural phenomena in Georgia life, and his part in the history of regionalism in America.

Kimball King

University of North Carolina at Chapel Hill

Acknowledgments

I wish to thank the following manuscript collections and librar-
ies for permitting me to quote from sections of Judge Longstreet's letters and other documents: the South Caroliniana
Library, Columbia, S. C.; the Dickinson College Library, Carlisle, Pa.; the R. W. Woodruff Library, Atlanta, Ga.; the Georgia
Historical Society, Atlanta, Ga.; the Robert Muldrow Cooper
Library, Clemson, S. C.; the Lilly Library, Bloomington, Ind.;
and the Library of Congress, Washington, D. C.

Muriel Dyer typed my original manuscript and David Steege,
my research assistant, has been a thoroughly conscientious proof-
reader.

Chronology

1790 Augustus Baldwin Longstreet born in Augusta, Georgia, on 22 September to William and Hannah Randolph Longstreet.

1808 Sent to the Waddell School in Willington, S. C., which John C. Calhoun had attended.

1811 Enters Yale as a junior.

1813 Graduates from Yale; studies law in Litchfield, Conn., at the school conducted by Judges Tapping Reeve and James Gould.

1815 Admitted to the Georgia bar on May 26; practices primarily in Richmond County.

1817 Marries Frances Eliza Parke on 3 March and moves into her family's home in Greensboro, Ga.; begins law practice in Green County.

1820 First child, Alfred Emsley, born in July. Daughter, born on Christmas Day of the following year. Both children die young and four others die in infancy. Two daughters, Frances Eliza and Virginia Lafayette, born in 1824 and 1826, survive to maturity.

1821 Elected representative to State Assembly from Greene County.

1822 Elected judge of the Superior Court of Ocmulgee District.

1824 Death of young son and Eliza Longstreet's mother causes Longstreet to withdraw from congressional elections.

1827 Joins Methodist Church with Mrs. Longstreet; Longstreet begins a law partnership with William

W. Mann, literary editor of *Southern Field and Fireside*, 1859, in Augusta, Ga.

1830 Begins writing sketches that later appear in *Georgia Scenes.*

1833 First sketch from *Georgia Scenes* published anonymously in the weekly *Southern Recorder*, Milledgeville, Ga. Nos. 2–7 follow at intervals, the last printed 15 January 1834.

1834 First issue published of *States Rights Sentinel*, owned and edited by Longstreet. Nos. 11–14 of *Georgia Scenes* printed, the last on 17 March 1835.

1835 *Georgia Scenes* by "a Native Georgian" published in book form by *Sentinel.*

1838 Enters the Methodist ministry.

1839 Gives up law practice for Augusta congregation; nurses sick during yellow fever epidemic. In August appointed president of Emory College.

1840 Harper's issues "second" edition of *Georgia Scenes* under author's name, with introduction and illustrations by E. H. Hyde.

1841 Awarded honorary degree of Doctor of Laws by Yale.

1842–1843 Uncollected sketches published in the *Magnolia, or Southern Monthly.*

1845 Pamphlet *Letters on the Epistle of Paul to Philemon or the Connection of Apostolical Christianity with Slavery* published in Charleston; daughter Frances marries Dr. Henry Branham.

1846 Writes letters from "Georgia" to "Massachusetts" on slavery issue. (Published in book form in 1847 as *A Voice from the South.*)

1847 Conducts the first religious revival in Atlanta with Bishop Andrews; daughter Virginia marries L. Q. C. Lamar.

1848 Resigns from Emory.

1849 Moves to Centenary College, Jackson, Louisiana,

but soon resigns; begins the story of *William Mitten,* the first five chapters of which are published in local weekly; elected president of the University of Mississippi.

1856 Offers resignation to Mississippi trustees 10 July but is refused 14 July. Receives degree of Doctor of Divinity 16 July. Again resigns on 17 July and decision is accepted.

1857 In November, elected president of South Carolina College.

1859 *Master William Mitten: Or a Youth of Brilliant Talents Who Was Ruined by Bad Luck* published serially in new weekly periodical, *Southern Field and Fireside,* 18 May–19 November. Published in book form in Macon, Ga., in 1864 and 1889.

1861 Writes antiwar protest, *Shall South Carolina Begin the War?* In November students at the University of South Carolina leave for war as a body and Longstreet returns to Mississippi. His nephew, James Longstreet, becomes a general.

1862 Home in Oxford, Miss., burned by Yankee soldiers.

1863 Lamars and Longstreets move first to Oxford, Ga., and then to Columbus, Ga.

1865 Longstreets leave Columbus and return to Oxford, Miss.

1867 Celebrates fiftieth wedding anniversary in March.

1868 In October wife Frances Eliza Parke Longstreet dies.

1869 Edward Mayes, Longstreet's friend and literary executor, marries his granddaughter, Frances Eliza Lamar.

1870 Dies a peaceful death on 9 July with his family around him in Oxford, Miss.

Chapter One

The Gifted Georgian

For Augustus Baldwin Longstreet, writing fiction was only one of many careers that he pursued successfully throughout his lifetime. Born in Augusta, Georgia, on 22 September 1790, he first practiced law and then served as a judge. Ultimately he became a clergyman and an educator, and authorship occupied only a small part of his time; he was already forty years old when he began to write his best known stories. Longstreet was a man of many talents who expected and received recognition for all his undertakings. He adhered to a classic ideal of well-roundedness. Wherever he directed his attention and energy, he earned respect for his intelligence, exuberance, and originality. As with many well-known men who seem to conquer new fields effortlessly, he often tired of his accomplishments before a more diligent and less versatile intelligence would have considered them complete.

So it was with Longstreet's foray into literature. Writing and collecting sketches during his tenure as a circuit court judge resulted in the hasty assembly of *Georgia Scenes,* which became an immediate success when it appeared as a book in 1835 and continued to impress readers with its vitality and freshness throughout the rest of the nineteenth century. In the twentieth century, it has been recognized as a classic of American humor. The author was gratified by the popularity of his first book but later considered writing comic anecdotes somewhat beneath his dignity. The man of letters was soon submerged in the man of affairs; the sheer force of his presence in his own time brought him more gratification than the dim promise of future literary renown. What is remarkable is that one flawed but charming book should earn a permanent place in American regional literature. Whether or not subsequent writers of middle Georgia, or of the whole South, were indebted personally to Longstreet's

I

example, they would frequently be compared to him if they recorded humorous southern folktales or told anecdotes of frontier life. Charles S. Syndor believes Longstreet started the vogue for southern folk writing,[1] and Edgar Allan Poe called the Judge's early sketches "a sure omen of better days for the literature of the South."[2]

Historians as well as literary critics have recognized Longstreet's importance in the antebellum South. Four times a college president, he was a model of moral strength and incorruptibility for several generations of educated southerners. In politics he was a staunch states' rights conservative, and as W. A. Cate has noted, "the teachings of the old Judge were to bear fruit in the large number of Emory men . . . who took leading parts in the Civil War."[3] Yet he bitterly opposed the war, although ironically his own invective against abolitionists and northern politicians may have contributed to the hostile prewar climate. Longstreet's nephew, James Longstreet, Lee's friend and a general in the war, and L. Q. C. Lamar, his son-in-law and the leading southern statesman after the war, first as senator, then as secretary of the interior and Supreme Court justice, both formed their political and religious convictions under the older man's vigilant tutelage. Lamar, who was nine years old when his own father committed suicide, attended Emory College during Longstreet's administration and became a lifelong admirer of the president. Like many young Georgians, Lamar discovered in his mentor a model of dynamic, responsible leadership.

For his own part, Longstreet, as Cate has observed, looked to young men as "the future saviors of the country."[4] His only novel, *William Mitten* (1855), based on his experience as teacher and administrator, reflects his interest in the psychology of adolescent development. He hoped that young, healthy, enlightened southerners could create an ideal society that the rest of the nation, perhaps even the world, might emulate. Georgia, in particular, could provide a second chance for American democracy because it was still unspoiled and unformed and could be nurtured, like a child, into a productive adulthood.

A Rough New Land

During the first forty-eight years of Longstreet's life, Georgia settlers battled Indians and pushed them off their lands. Although the state had been among the original thirteen colonies, it was one of the last on the Atlantic coast to develop a stable society. Most of the state was heavily wooded and uninhabitable, and the average Georgian was impoverished and lived in a shanty. While the cultivation of cotton and slavery in the more prosperous areas discouraged small farmers from immigrating, the big plantations had very little capital because of the difficulty of transporting cotton over the rough roads, swollen rivers, and swamps of the raw countryside. Industries, small businesses, and jobs for middle-class people were slow to develop. The inhabitants of this rough territory were frequently desperate and lawless. The Duc de la Rochefoucauld-Liancourt wrote in his *Travels through the United States of America* that Georgia was an utterly chaotic area and its inhabitants the most lazy, disorderly, and drunken that he had ever seen. Still, Rochefoucauld claims they had the energy to rob and kill the Indians and cheat them out of their remaining lands.[5] Furthermore, these roughnecks were all inveterate fighters and often mutilated themselves and others for life by their biting, clawing, and kicking. One sketch in Longstreet's *Georgia Scenes,* "The Fight," describes a contest in which one young pugilist bites off another's nose while he, himself, loses an ear. Longstreet's tone is nearly slapstick, so that his story takes on the aspect of a tall tale. Where Rochefoucauld had shuddered at the violent and grotesque aspects of country life, Longstreet took an amusedly tolerant view of frontier hell raising.

The government of Georgia wanted to encourage permanent settlers of a higher type, but most of their methods were counterproductive. Just after the Revolution, every veteran had been promised two hundred free acres of land, plus additional land for the other members of his family. After 1800 the state began a series of land lotteries in which citizens could draw for additional property. During the first third of the nineteenth century, there were eight major land distributions, involving more than twenty million acres. A high percentage of this land was purchased by speculators who took large profits for themselves and cheated thousands of ordinary people. The state was ultimately the loser, but a few rapacious individuals became enormously rich.[6]

In 1750, when Georgia acquired the territory between the Ogeechee and Oconee rivers from the Creek Indian tribe, settlers quickly moved into the fertile northernmost parts of this area, but the lands to the south were completely unsuited to farming. Georgians referred to the lower area as the "pine barrens." Although pine trees, gray-colored long moss, and sandy soil provided diversion for adventurous hunters, agriculture and community life in such an area seemed unfeasible. Opportunists recognized the possibilities of acquiring, then unloading, this worthless land to northeastern or foreign business interests who found ready customers in the influx of unsuspecting immigrants arriving daily from Europe. One of the chief promoters of what Thomas P. Abernethy has called "Pine Barren" speculation was Senator James Gunn of Georgia. Gunn's spokesman and manager in the legislature was Longstreet's father, William. In 1795 William Longstreet received one of ten shares in the Georgia Company, which had claimed huge areas of Georgia wasteland.[7] At the time, Augustus Longstreet was barely five years old. Legislative battles over the legality of this and other land transactions prevented any clear-cut disposition of the property for fifteen years until March of 1810, when the Supreme Court finally ruled in favor of the speculators. Meanwhile the original company shares had changed hands many times. It is not known whether the elder Longstreet profited from the eventual disposition of the case. If so, he may have ventured his gains on some less lucrative project, since he never became a wealthy man.

In the more fertile areas, the first settlers of Georgia planted mostly corn and some tobacco along the edges of the Savannah River. There were a few rice plantations in the swampy areas. By 1800, however, cotton had become the state's primary crop. Most of the produce was shipped out from Savannah, which became a center of the trade. In the first two decades of the nineteenth century, a planter could buy slaves and make a substantial profit on cotton. By the 1830s, however, the best soil had already been destroyed by cultivation of the crop, and the price of cotton fell to the point where agriculture became unprofitable. Planters who could afford to buy out their neighbors did so. Thus, most of the small, independent farmers either were driven from their profession or else decided to move farther west. In "The Turn-Out," which Longstreet wrote for the *Southern Recorder* in 1833 and which was later included in *Georgia Scenes,* Hall, the narrator, laments the destruction of the beautiful countryside in what was first called Richmond, later Columbia, County. He tells how a local farmer once said to him, "These lands will never wear out." Then Hall adds how greatly altered this landscape was to become over a period of forty years:

The sun poured his whole strength upon the bald hill which once supported the sequestered schoolhouse; many a deepwashed gully met at a sickly bog where gushed the limpid fountain; a dying willow rose from the soil which nourished the venerable beech; flocks wandered among the dwarf grass and cropped a scanty meal from the vale where the rich cane bowed and rustled to every breeze, and all around was barren, dreary, and cheerless.[8]

Passages such as this are rare in Longstreet's early works, which generally present a positive view of country life. Later the destruction of land and houses in the war would surround him with more desolate landscapes.

The Longstreet Family Adventure

After the Revolution, there had been a mass migration of settlers mainly from Virginia and North Carolina who pushed into Indian territory across virgin land in hopes of creating a better society. Some, as Davy Crockett has related, were refugees from justice,[9] and Longstreet ascribes such a background to the political upstart, Darby Anvil, in a story he wrote in 1839. Others, like the Longstreet family, were well-established members of other communities but welcomed adventure and the promises of greater prosperity. Still, Longstreet's mother, the former Hannah Randolph of Princeton, New Jersey, must have had moments when she wondered how she could have left the amenities of the Northeast to trek across rough Georgia roads to a remote country village. Doubtless, the prospect of limitless servants was appealing to the future mother of six, and the money she had inherited from her father, James Randolph, would have more purchasing power in the South. It has been noted that Longstreet's father, William, attempted to profit from the land grants of the 1790s. His family, the Langestraets of Dutch descent, had lived for five generations in the North. Like many Americans William cherished the dream of

becoming rich and famous as an inventor, perhaps like Ben
Franklin. He was an educated man with scientific interests. Once
he invented a steamboat which traveled five miles up the Savannah River a few days before Fulton's boat made its successful
trip,[10] and he built two steam-driven cotton gins, which were
destroyed by fire, as well as a steam mill wrecked in the War
of 1812.

William Longstreet was extremely sensitive to criticism of
his failed inventions, which had resulted in major financial losses
as well as damaged pride. One time he took his young son,
Gus, to the theater and in surprise and anger heard one of
the actors singing a satirical composition about an absurd-looking
boat Longstreet was in the process of constructing. It is not
certain that Gus was even aware that the object of the actor's
satire was his own father. All he knew was that his outraged
companion dragged him from his seat and that the two of them
marched out of the theater to the amazement of others in the
audience. John Donald Wade in his biography, *Augustus Baldwin
Longstreet: A Study of the Development of Culture in the South,* believes this episode left its mark on young Gus. From the moment
when the boy left the theater with his agitated father, he fancied
that the most effective form of retaliation to any insult was to
make a dramatic and stately withdrawal from the offender's society. Wade suggests that this early flight from the theater initiated
a predictable reaction to stress which became part of Longstreet's
character; however, it could also be considered normal behavior
for a self-confident person who believed the loss of his own
company constituted a major deprivation to any gathering. In
any event, Gus Longstreet had a highly developed sense of
the dramatic, an ability to draw attention to himself which was
very useful to a politician, clergyman, and teacher.

In spite of the fact that William Longstreet's money-making
schemes were generally as unsuccessful as his inventions, his
family maintained a fairly high position in Georgia society. They
were educated beyond the level of the average Georgian and
owned property and slaves. The first pioneers (called "crackers"
by the residents of the more prosperous seacoast areas because
the main staple of their diet was cracked corn) were hardworking
homesteaders. By 1830, however, there were only a few small
landowners, and "crackers" was a derisive term, describing un-

skilled white families caught in a hopeless cycle of poverty. The slaves at the bottom of the social structure appeared to many outsiders more hopeful and contented than the crackers. Travelers from abroad compared their lot favorably to that of the European working class, but they would not, as tourists, have observed the abuses of the system and would have overlooked the long-term psychological damage of forced servitude.

It is difficult to know how Gus perceived his own family's status in relation to the rest of Georgia society. He knew that, as a small community judged such things, the Longstreets stood above the crackers and the blacks, but he was aware of tensions over family finances. His fascination with people of great wealth or of political power was probably inculcated in him at an early age by his ambitious but unsuccessful father.

In later life he cherished his associations with the rich and the famous. His correspondence to family members often alluded to his contacts with distinguished people and even in his fiction he included lengthy digressions on the ancestry of distinguished persons. His alter ego, Captain Thompson in *William Mitten,* stressed that his nephew should cultivate friendships with boys from established Georgia and Carolina families.

Young Gus

Even at an early age Gus was extremely competitive, measuring everything he did against other boys' standards. As he later wrote of the happy years he spent on a South Carolina farm near Augusta between 1805 and 1810, "My highest ambition was to out-run, out-jump, out-shoot, throw down and whip, any man in the district, and I was giving fair promise of attaining my end."[11] All of his family attested to his energy, ambition, and precocity. When he was seven, his mother described his talents to a friend: "You ask about little Augustus. Well, I must tell you he is one of the finest boys you ever saw. He goes to school, reads and writes, and often makes observations that would surprise you for a child of his age,—was his father's Pett till William come [*sic*], but now his nose is out of joint."[12]

When she wrote this letter, Mrs. Longstreet already had five sons and two daughters. Like many children in large families, Gus was often forced to make a spectacle of himself in order to gain attention. He was neither handsome nor graceful, but he had a sense of his own worth and knew how to command attention. In school he was noted for his ability to make grotesque grimaces with one side of his face while keeping the side toward the schoolmaster perfectly still. He was recognized as a disruptive influence on the other students and spent hours on the dunce stool, where he was in a perfect position to continue his clowning. He gained additional notice by failing to complete his homework or by giving flawed, even comical recitations. His attention-gaining tactics were so effective that one of his teachers suggested to his parents that he might be insane.

Longstreet's family believed that Gus first began to outgrow his need for negative recognition when he discovered the friendship of a red-headed country boy named George McDuffie, who would one day become governor of South Carolina. McDuffie went to work for a local storekeeper in order to help out his impoverished family. He boarded with the Longstreets and shared a room with Gus. Although McDuffie was not brilliant or good-looking, his tremendous self-discipline, his yearning to improve himself through hard work and study, and his openness to new ideas provided Gus with a wholesome image of young manhood. Longstreet identified with McDuffie, whose struggle to the top would be more arduous than his own, and years later described his admiration for the boy in *William Mitten.* There he would be the model for John Brown, who would be portrayed as sharing many of Longstreet's own qualities. Soon the boys began to study together, and by 1808 when Longstreet was sent to Dr. Moses Waddel's school at Willington, South Carolina, his study habits had improved. In Willington he boarded with William Calhoun, John C. Calhoun's brother, who looked up McDuffie at Longstreet's suggestion and took an interest in him, placing him also at Dr. Waddel's.

The boys graduated from Dr. Waddel's in 1811, entering their respective colleges as juniors, and they always thought of their years at Willington as pleasant and mentally invigorating. Longstreet described the school in *William Mitten:*

There was a street shaded by majestic oaks and composed entirely of log huts varying in size from six to seven feet square. . . . This street was about forty yards wide and its length was perhaps double its width, and the houses on either side did not number more than ten or twelve; of course, therefore, they stood in very open order. They were all built by the students themselves or by architects of their hiring. They served for study houses in cold or rainy weather, though the students were allowed to study where they pleased within convenient reach of the monitors.[13]

The students boarded in houses nearby and were encouraged to do seasonal chores. They usually cut their own firewood and built their own fires. Longstreet enjoyed the freedom of caring for himself in this peaceful rural community and wrote, "When studying the classics under the shade of the beautiful beeches which grew near the woodland seat of science, I actually felt a touch of the inspiration with which Virgil opens his deathless song."[14] The boys' exercises in debate were practical training for the legal profession, and as pranksters they argued such topics as: "Whether, at public elections, should the votes of faction predominate by internal suggestions, or the bias of jurisprudence?" a topic recorded in Longstreet's story "The Debate." Later in life McDuffie, Longstreet, and the other boys were to become quite sentimental about their experiences in Waddel's school.

Longstreet valued loyalty in friendship and throughout his life maintained relationships begun in his childhood. The early respect and admiration of his friends left him with a desire to make a significant contribution to his community. As he grew to manhood, his lanky frame filled out to give him an imposing presence. He was still prone to clowning or grimacing when he experienced embarrassment, but increasingly he relied on the kind of forthright dignity he had observed in McDuffie if he wished to command respect.

College and a Career

Although Longstreet's parents remembered Princeton University with affection, they were close friends of the Calhoun family in nearby South Carolina and of John C. Calhoun, in particular, who had graduated from Yale in 1804. In the same year that Longstreet graduated from Waddel's school, John C. Calhoun took a seat in Congress and married his cousin, Floride

Bouneau, who owned a large plantation in Abbeville, South Carolina. With the encouragement and support of Henry Clay, who arranged for him to be chairman of the Committee on Foreign Affairs, Calhoun became a major spokesman for the southern "War Hawks," who favored annexation of Florida and Texas and who helped commit the country to the War of 1812. An admirer of Calhoun, young Longstreet wished to matriculate at Yale as the statesman had done, and Longstreet's parents approved the choice. William Longstreet perhaps saw the opportunity for his son to flatter Calhoun and to strengthen a family connection that would be valuable in later life. He recognized that Gus had the potential to achieve the recognition and wealth he himself had sought. Some immediate financial sacrifice was involved, and none of the other Longstreet children was offered a similar opportunity. Mainly it was the children of the very rich in the South who went to Harvard, Yale, or Princeton. Ordinary families feared the scorn of their neighbors for appearing disloyal to the regional universities. The impoverished John Brown in *William Mitten* attended Princeton but his tuition was paid by local aristocrats who recognized and rewarded his fine character and mental gifts. Possibly some of William Longstreet's friends contributed to Gus's expenses, maybe even the Calhouns, though there is no record of any scholarship help for the boy. Gus realized that he had been singled out for distinction, however, and was aware of both the privileges and responsibilities of a Yale education.

Although at Waddel's he had been respected by his classmates as well as by adults for his intelligence and ambition, he feared he lacked the social finesse or grace to impress the sophisticated young men he expected to find in New Haven. During his teen years, he had grown tall so quickly that he seemed awkward, not quite in control of his movements or gestures. He worried about his blemished adolescent complexion, his unruly hair, his excessive thinness. With his Georgia drawl and mean wardrobe of hand-me-downs, he was instantly recognized as a country bumpkin. A Georgian was a comic stereotype to many Yankees, who believed Georgians were made up of outcasts from Virginia and the Carolinas. Gus could have stressed the genteel New Jersey background of his grandparents in conversations with his new friends or he might have impressed them with the Dutch descent he shared with many of the New York boys at Yale. He chose instead to present himself as a plain-speaking country boy, who nonetheless valued intellectual pursuits. Even though he was comfortable working in a cornfield, he also read Latin poetry for relaxation. Rather than permitting snobbish students to make jokes about his lack of polish, he told jokes on himself, accentuating his drawl and selecting details of small-town life designed to amuse and intrigue worldly northerners.

When other students casually discussed their rich relatives or friends in government, Gus would mention his close friend John Calhoun's recent achievements on the Committee on Foreign Affairs; and he detailed his own plans for a career in politics. At the same time, however, he was being exposed to students and teachers who actively criticized books and writing. Timothy Dwight was the president of Yale, and many on the campus were well aware of his reputation as one of the "Connecticut Wits." Along with John Trumbull and Joel Barlow, Dwight had been famous for poetry that celebrated American literary independence. Longstreet may have read *Greenfield Hill* and *The Conquest of Canaan* and was possibly moved by the poet's vision of the simple, pious life. Joel Barlow's "Hasty Pudding" was another poem well known to Yale students in Longstreet's day, and its comical description of concocting a traditional New England mush recipe would have appealed to Longstreet's sense of humor and appreciation for folk traditions. Also in a humorous vein was Trumbull's *M'Fingal,* which combined the history of the American Revolution with the satirical technique of Samuel Butler's *Hudibras.*

There is no evidence that Longstreet himself attempted to write satire or verse at this time, but he may have gained a new respect for literature during his New Haven years. In the variety of his pursuits, he would come to resemble President Dwight, the grandson of Jonathan Edwards, who, like his forbear, was a Calvinist preacher. Dwight combined college administration with an active ministry and a career in letters; his versatility amazed the students who jokingly referred to him as the "Pope." Probably no one would have guessed in 1811 and 1812 that Gus Longstreet's life would someday run a close parallel to old Pope Dwight's. When he graduated from Yale in 1813, Longstreet continued to follow in Calhoun's footsteps and entered the law school run by Judges Tapping Reeve and James Gould in Litchfield, Connecticut. At Litchfield he took notes on various phases of the law which he later transformed into ledgers; these were to become his principal guide in the years when he would practice law.

Longstreet found Litchfield slightly less friendly than New Haven had been. In college he had been part of a small privileged community that was self-contained and protected. He appreciated the charm of Litchfield but evidently felt like more of an outsider in a somewhat stern puritan environment. Attending the Reverend Ward Beecher's sermons, he was mildly offended by the clergyman's fierce, egotistical manner. Emily Vanderpool, who wrote chronicles of the law school at Litchfield, comments that although Longstreet objected to Beecher, he was fond of one of his daughters (not Harriet, she hastens to add). He also found time to visit Miss Pierce's School for Young Ladies, where he frequently regaled the young women with his droll accounts of rural Georgia in his "country boy" pose. His first practice as a raconteur began during the Connecticut years, when he established his individuality in part by flaunting his southern background. He perceived the potential liability of his provincial heritage and turned it into a unique asset.

William Longstreet died in 1814 and his son returned to Georgia. Absence from his home state had added to the young man's affection for it. Now that he had completed his education and his father was gone, he took charge of his own life with particular determination. He began in earnest to prepare for his bar examinations and passed them on 26 May 1815. He was grateful that his father had encouraged him to go to Yale and law school and vowed to make good use of his training, proving to his community that the older Longstreet's faith in his unusual abilities was justified and gaining a prominence in southern affairs that would distinguish the entire Longstreet family.

Thus, at the age of about twenty-five, Longstreet began riding the Richmond County circuit as a lawyer. The center of his practice was Augusta, by that time a city of over six thousand people in a county of more than fifteen thousand (about one-third were slaves), but his profession took him into the surrounding towns and even nearby Greene County. In Greensboro he met Frances Eliza Parke, the daughter of well-to-do parents, who was nine years younger than he and from all accounts a refined, intelligent, quiet person with the qualities Longstreet believed a southern woman should possess. According to Wade, she was "small, graceful, and exceptionally pretty, not only charming in manners and able to quote poetry to fit any occasion, but punctilious in the performance of every duty that her time, which demanded very much of a woman, taught her pertained to a housewife."[15] L. Q. C. Lamar, her son-in-law, wrote in his effusive way that she was the non-pareil of woman, "full of warmth and tenderness and depth of feeling, confiding, trustworthy, a lover of home, a true wife and mother, whose hand touched and beautified and sanctified all domestic relations."[16]

She was married to Longstreet on 3 March 1817 at the age of eighteen, and they lived together until she died fifty-one years later. Her husband wrote after her death, "In all this time I do not believe that she ever uttered one word or did one thing to wound my feelings." He added in this same letter, "She, as you know, had a very handsome estate when I married her; I did not have money enough to buy my wedding clothes."[17] It has also been said that Longstreet was unable to pay the clergyman who performed their marriage ceremony any kind of honorarium, much to that gentleman's annoyance; a few months later, however, Longstreet, meeting this same clergyman in a clothing store, insisted on buying him an entire outfit. Longstreet's father had left property to each of his children, but Longstreet had transferred the title of his share worth $3,000 to one of his brothers before his marriage. In any case, his wife's property was perhaps as much as ten times this sum.

The circumstances of the Longstreets' early married life followed the pattern of the groom's parents' relationship since Hannah Randolph Longstreet had been an heiress and she and William were dependent on her parents during their years in Princeton. It seemed natural, then, to Gus that his wife's fortune could provide luxuries for them that he himself could not yet afford. Theirs was a love match but the young Longstreets were equally aware of the practical benefits of Frances's money on Gus's professional advancement. During the first year of their marriage, the young couple lived with the bride's family; then they purchased a six-hundred-acre farm nearby for $6,000 where

Longstreet raised horses and grafted fruit trees, one of his life-long hobbies. The major sadness in their married life was Mrs. Longstreet's delicate health and the fact that only two daughters out of eight children lived to maturity. Longstreet was known as a family man, and although he and his wife moved from place to place with considerable frequency in their later years, they enjoyed the presence of both married daughters with their families either in the same town or in the same house. A well-run family was, in Longstreet's opinion, a necessary microcosm of any worthwhile civilization. His own provided him with continuous support, and perhaps his bonds to relatives were especially close because he formed few truly deep relationships with friends in his maturity and had no tolerance for friendly criticism. He was too competitive and opinionated to put acquaintances at ease. Yet, interestingly, his sons-in-law, who were equally ambitious, loyally defended him at all times and seemed to feel a genuine affection for him, suggesting that he had a warmth or appeal that made him more than just an impressive authority figure to those who knew him best.

At home Longstreet enjoyed having an audience for his humorous stories and his musical talents on the flute; he had a quick ear and could pick out a tune with ease, entertaining his friends, students, grandchildren. He became famous for storytelling, and of Longstreet's droll yarns, a colleague at Centenary College said, "He was inimitable as a story-teller . . . no one could resist the contagion of his humor. He was usually the center of a listening, laughing, admiring crowd."[18]

The background for many of these stories lay in Longstreet's early experiences in the circuit courts where from 1822 to 1825 he served a term as judge of the Superior Court of the Ocmulgee District. There was a fraternal spirit among the judges and lawyers who rode the circuit. Away from their families, they gathered in taverns and swapped amusing stories of rural life. Local characters and unusual court cases became legendary and each storyteller vied with his peers in making his version of a tale the most humorous or exciting. One of Longstreet's contemporaries gives the following account of circuit riding and the life of a frontier judge:

Our circuit consisted of seven counties, and the ridings were spring and fall, occupying about two months each term. In each courthouse town was a tavern or two. These houses of entertainment were not then dignified with the sonorous title of hotel. The proprietors were usually jolly good fellows, or some staid matronly lady, in black gown and blue cap, and they all looked forward with anxious delight to the coming of court week. Every preparation was made for the judge and lawyers. Beds were aired and the bugs turned out. . . . The room usually appropriated to the Bench and Bar was a great vagabond-hall, denominated the ball-room, and for this purpose appropriated once or twice a year. Along the bare walls of this mighty dormitory were arranged beds, each usually occupied by a couple of the limbs of the law, and sometimes appropriated to three. If there was not a spare apartment, a bed was provided here for the judge. . . . Here assembled at night the rollicking boys of the Georgia Bar, who here indulged, without restraint, the convivialities for which they were so celebrated. Humor and wit, in anecdote and repartee, beguiled the hours. . . . [How fine it was to enjoy] a night in one of these old tumble-down rooms, with A. S. Clayton, O. H. Prince, A. B. Longstreet and John M. Dooley . . . [all] chosen spirits of fun![19]

The year preceding his appointment as judge, Longstreet had been elected representative to the state assembly from Greene County, whose population was approximately the same as Richmond County's, and he had been elected captain of the 398th district company of the Georgia Militia. He was the leader he had trained to be in his profession and in his community.

The Death of a Son

Longstreet prepared to run in the congressional elections of 1824 and seemed to have excellent prospects of winning. His friendship with John Calhoun was widely known and Calhoun was campaigning at this same time to become vice-president. Enthusiasm for Calhoun's candidacy in the South might have facilitated Longstreet's own bid for office. However, early in the fall of 1824, his wife's mother and his son suddenly died within two days of each other. Little Alfred Longstreet had been a healthy child, and his death at four was the first major heartbreak of his parents' lives. Always deeply involved in the life of his family, Longstreet had not been a detached father, assigning all child-rearing duties to his wife. In all his stories of family life, the male protagonists are actively involved with shaping young lives, providing examples and encouraging independence. Sometimes these father figures are severe or self-righteous, but they are never too concerned with their profession or pleasure to shirk their responsibilities toward their offspring. Longstreet fell into a deep depression after the child's funeral and was placed under a physician's care. Although he continued as judge and his wife bore more children, most of whom would also die, Longstreet does seem to have changed fundamentally from this time. There was always afterwards a restless, melancholy quality about him. He had many adventures and literary and academic achievements, but he never seems to have been the open, joyful person that had delighted the students at Dr. Waddel's, the young ladies in Litchfield, or the "boys of the Georgia Bar."

His wife's stepfather, Ebenezer Torrance, a devout Methodist, was one source of strength and comfort to him during this period, and after more than two years of prayer and soul-searching, Longstreet and his wife joined the Methodist Church. At about this time, he and his family moved to Augusta and bought a plantation outside the city; he became a local preacher the following year and a leading advocate of the temperance movement in spite of its northern ties to abolition and the fact that he, although fierce in his abhorrence of drunkenness, was not a teetotaler but enjoyed a glass of wine. He devoted more and more time to religious causes when, after a three-year term, he failed to be re-elected to a judgeship because of political infighting. This disappointment, coupled with his continued grieving over his son's death, brought his political career to an end. He was, however, engaged in an active law partnership with William W. Mann (later to be literary editor of the *Southern Field and Fireside,* which published *William Mitten* serially), and they were joined by Charles J. Jenkins in 1833.

During this time, Longstreet kept up with his business investments, increased his involvement in church activities, and began to publish the sketches of *Georgia Scenes,* which were first printed pseudonymously under the names of "Hall" and "Baldwin." Earlier he had written some poetry and a legal article, now lost, "A Review of the Decision of the Supreme Court of the United States in the Case of McCulloch vs. the State of Maryland."

It is not known what his review of the court decision contained except that its tone was generally negative. *McCulloch* v. *Maryland* was a case resulting in a decision by the Supreme Court to uphold the constitutionality of the Second Bank of the United States. It was a milestone in American nationalism and Chief Justice Marshall's argument for the majority in which he declared that Congress had the "implied powers" to establish the bank was generally considered his most brilliant constitutional opinion. His opponents, of course, feared that such powers might easily be abused. Longstreet may have worried that the "implied powers" would interfere with states' rights. Sixteen years later in a letter to Calhoun, dated 4 July 1848, on quite a different subject, he digressed to express his long-standing disapproval of the *McCulloch* decision, noting:

Congress had not the *constitutional* power to establish a bank, the decision of the Supreme Court rest [*sic*] upon the single principle; that Congress may create an agency to accomplish a given power, and a bank is a suitable agency to manage its fiscal concerns. The difficulty with the argument is that a Bank is no agent of the government, or it could not maintain an existence independent of it, as the old U. S. Bank did after Jackson removed the deposits. Here was an *agent* that had no more connection with the government than I had.[20]

Longstreet always adhered strictly to the Constitution as it was written; his later essays on the racial issue discuss constitutional provisions very literally. While he was expressing his annoyance at the court's decision in the National Bank's expansion, he was also urging full support of Calhoun's Ordinance of Nullification. Calhoun, then vice-president, had been angered by the protective tariff of 1828, which he had called the tariff of abominations, and for the next four years, he used his influence in Washington and South Carolina to persuade the South Carolina legislature to draft the Ordinance of Nullification. His public split with President Andrew Jackson over the tariff issue led him to resign the vice-presidency late in 1832 after he had been safely elected senator from South Carolina. Jackson countered nullification with the Force Bill in 1833, in which he maintained that bearing arms to resist a government order, as the Ordinance of Nullification had proposed, was an act of treason.

A national crisis was averted when Jackson and Calhoun negotiated many of their differences in the compromise tariff of 1833. Nevertheless, southern bitterness over the issue failed to abate, and Longstreet was one of many public figures who continued to rail at government tariffs and interference with regional sovereignty. American legal issues tended only to increase Longstreet's general state of depression, and his family and friends hoped to turn his mind to new projects. Perhaps with their encouragement, he began consigning to paper the anecdotes he was noted for telling. The first sketches were printed in 1833–34 in the weekly Milledgeville *Southern Recorder:* "The Dance" was published first, followed by "The Song," "The Horse Swap," "The Turf," "The Fight," "The Turn-Out," "The Character of a Native Georgian," and "The Gander Pulling."

In 1834 Longstreet decided to try his hand at newspaper publishing and became owner-editor of the *States Rights Sentinel,* an Augusta weekly. For the next two years, until he sold the *Sentinel* to the *Chronicle*'s editor, William E. Jones, and the two papers merged as Augusta's first daily, Longstreet used his paper to express his opinions on politics and morals. His comments, signed "Bob Short," included a strong stand on nullification with a states rights bias and propaganda supporting the temperance movement. The name "Short" appealed to Longstreet because he was fond of jokes about his tall, lanky stature and also because it was an antonym to the first syllable of his actual surname.[21]

He continued printing "Hall's" and "Baldwin's" sketches on Georgia frontier life. "The Charming Creature as a Wife," "Militia Drill" (by O. H. Prince), "The Mother and Her Child," "The Fox Hunt," "The Wax Works," "The Debating Society," and "A Sage Conversation" appeared in the *Sentinel,* as well as "Dropping to Sleep," which was not included in the collection published in book form in 1835. Again, in this publication, the author was unnamed, identified simply with the phrase "By a Native Georgian." The other four sketches included in *Georgia Scenes*—"Georgia Theatrics," "The Ball," "An Interesting Interview," and "The Shooting Match"—were printed in the *States Rights Sentinel.* There were also some other, uncollected stories published later in the *Augusta Mirror* and the *Magnolia* which were published posthumously in *Stories with a Moral* (1912). The sketches that appeared in *Georgia Scenes* were brought out in a second edition by Harper's in 1840 under Longstreet's name and with an introduction by the author. The volume won critical acclaim in the North and South, and just at the time when Longstreet's interest in the law was flagging— his last important legal case was argued before the state Supreme Court in January 1839—he gained a national reputation as an author of the Georgia frontier.

Longstreet's Interest in Writing Subsides

Along with the Judge's other admirers, Frances Eliza Longstreet was immensely proud of *Georgia Scenes*. Although some of the stories may have been too crude for her taste, she recognized a quality of genius in the book that she herself had nurtured. Augustus had always had an instinctive sense of comic timing; he could weave the many threads of his stories into a colorful homespun tapestry. Furthermore, he was an excellent mimic and careful observer of idiosyncrasies of speech and manner. Responding to an appreciative gathering, he would become actor as well as storyteller, first winning the trust of his audience and then teasing and surprising them. His wife played her own part in these entertainments since she was adept at leading the conversation toward subjects that were natural starting points for the Judge's anecdotes, and she showed special preference for guests who begged their host for a story. If Frances blushed, Augustus might temper his language or restrain his tendency toward earthiness; just as often he would respond by making his story more improbable or even saltier. Her raised eyebrow could signal disapproval—or provocation. Thus, she became a kind of director for his performances.

When Longstreet had first started writing down the stories that had enlivened dinner parties and family gatherings, his wife hoped that this new vocation might provide an antidote to the growing restlessness she had observed for some years. Neither law, farming, politics, nor newspaper publishing had been able to absorb what she considered an alarming excess of energy. She guessed that he had not yet reconciled himself to little Alfred's death and that, like herself, he probably never would. She was encouraged that he wrote easily, that his written words so successfully captured the mood of the original anecdote. When he began submitting his stories to the *Sentinel,* he could barely contain himself until he saw them on the printed page. Then, immediately, he closeted himself in his study and began another. Always obsessive, Augustus subordinated all his other activities to this new interest for about a year. But when the stories were finally combined into one book, a book that would mark the beginning of his literary career, he mysteriously lost his fervor. Frances clipped favorable notices and reviews out of journals, relayed the compliments of friends and strangers, and daily expressed her pride in his newest accomplishment. Longstreet's passion to write, however, quickly spent itself, and just as in the past when he had mastered each new challenge and received his reward, so now he felt inexplicably disappointed and dissatisfied.

No one has yet explained convincingly why *Georgia Scenes,* which would set in motion a whole school of southern writing, failed to inspire its own author to duplicate his success. Hubbell and others, in arguing that the Judge may have been embarrassed by his own rough yarns, have underestimated both his prideful nature and his lifelong fondness for down-to-earth values. A more perceptive evaluation of Longstreet's behavior in general was offered by an Ohioan named Charles Reemelin, who entered into a magazine debate with Longstreet on religious matters, and who commented perspicaciously about his author friend:

Judge Longstreet's strength and his weakness . . . lie in this: his intensification in all things. The first, because he espouses every cause with sincere fervor; the second because his zeal obscures his vision, so that he sees both too much and too little of any subject which, for the time being, engages his mind.[22]

According to Wade, Longstreet confirmed the veracity of Reemelin's observation. In the particular case of *Georgia Scenes,* however, it is more likely he failed to find in writing the kind of gratification that personal responses to his storytelling had once brought him. While he appreciated the importance of self-control and intellectual discipline, he had not yet found, and never could find, a project or cause that would become a permanent commitment. Only to his family and his native region would he prove his unequivocal devotion and loyalty. Although he must have perceived the virtues of being a good husband and father, he discovered no heroism in this role; he would like to have been known for his valor, but he had been born too early to become a hero in the South's stand for independence. His ability to love, protect, and encourage those closest to him was his most impressive gift, but there is no reason to believe he ever consciously valued it as such.

Halfheartedly, Longstreet composed a few sketches for his friend, William Tappan Thompson, editor of the *Augusta Mirror,* during the three years following the publication of *Georgia Scenes.* Yet Thompson, as well as Mrs. Longstreet and the Judge's friends, began to realize that he had lost the urgency to express himself in print and that he was again preparing to pledge himself to a new career. He had experienced the physical challenge of farm work and the intellectual challenge of practicing law and writing a book; now the spiritual challenge of the ministry summoned him.

A Call to Duty

He had converted to Methodism in 1827, three years after his son's death, but his decision to become a minister came some ten years later. He was admitted to the ministry in January 1839 and, after more than three years probation as pastor and preacher, became a deacon and the following year an elder. Of his decision to give up politics and enter the ministry, he wrote the following recollection of a conversation with his wife:

My dear wife, I feel that I am under the last call of God to preach his gospel. So far as it concerns me personally it will cost me no effort to obey it, but when I think of *you,* I recoil from it. A man may be a lawyer and a true Christian, but I am satisfied that he cannot be a practicing attorney and an efficient preacher at the same time. If, therefore, I enter the ministry, I shall abandon the law. . . . But what is to become of you? You have never enjoyed three months of unbroken health since I first knew you. You must bid adieu to this spacious, peaceful country-seat, with all its sacred associations (we had buried two children near it) and its comfortable surroundings, to follow your husband to all places and all classes of people, where and with whom he may be ordered to work for God. How can you endure such a life, after the life of ease and affluence that you have always led?[23]

Longstreet did not provide the text of his wife's response except to note she supported his decision. He might have been overdramatizing the hardships of his new career, since anyone in the church hierarchy aware of Longstreet's position in society and his business assets would not send him far from home; for example, he and Mrs. Longstreet would most probably not have been considered as potential candidates for missionary duties in the mountains to the west.

In fact, Longstreet's first position as a clergyman was in Augusta, where the congregation numbered about six hundred, but he had to deal that first summer with a fierce yellow fever epidemic. For five long months, he ministered to his people, visiting and nursing the sick. He turned his own home on the outskirts of town into a hospital and worked with the Roman Catholic priest, John Barry, who also took fever victims into his home. The two men grew very close during this crisis, and Longstreet recorded their association with warmth: "At first we met with friendly salutations, then with a few words of conversation, . . . and finally with mutual demonstrations of brotherly love which, I believe, were sincere on both sides."[24] On one occasion Longstreet was called to the hospital by Father Barry to minister to one of the former judge's own congregation, and the two clergymen, priest and pastor, prayed together beside the sick man. In Longstreet's words, "I knelt, and Barry knelt with me, and at the conclusion of the prayer we sent our *Amens* to heaven together."[25] This friendship with a priest, as well as his late conversion to orthodox Christianity, may have influenced his tolerant views toward his fellow Christians of other denominations. His conservative politics, however, had been bred in the bone. Since earliest youth, he had been associated with the most conservative politicians of Georgia and South Carolina, rather than with the more liberal unionist wing, which was strongly represented in Georgia right up to the war. This blend of liberal religious views and reactionary political attitudes reveal his complex and questing nature.

A New Career

In August 1839, Longstreet was asked to become the president of Emory College, incorporated two years earlier, in Oxford, Georgia. Bishop Oscar P. Fitzgerald suggests that the Methodist trustees of the infant institution were more impressed with Longstreet's religious views than with his literary or legal achievement:

Doubtless the prime consideration with the trustees in his election was the desire to utilize his great popularity and influence in behalf of the movement to lay broad and deep and strong the foundations of a Christian college under the control of the Methodist denomination in Georgia.[26]

It seems likely that his varied talents and his wide reputation made Longstreet an ideal candidate for the position. It is true that in a sense Longstreet's life was spent in service to others, and the private man was always his happiest performing public duties. Wade describes his presence as imposing, a quality that doubtlessly enhanced his position at Emory: "He was tall and spare with an easy, graceful carriage, and though much has been said of his homeliness of countenance, he was of such magnetic personality that he was rather attractive than otherwise. He had fair complexion, brown hair, blue eyes, and a large, rather flexible mouth."[27]

Others found him stiff and awkward, however; a student who heard one of his sermons in the Methodist church complained that he was a boring and graceless preacher and that his theology was oddly eclectic. It is true that he insisted upon total immersion at his own baptism, which other Methodists generally frowned on, and he horrified the antipapists with his constant use of Latin. His prayers, said one parishioner, were rendered in "a very cold, conversational manner."[28] Still he was admired by Bishop James O. Andrew and other leaders of the Methodist church, such as Lovick and George Pierce, who had influenced Longstreet to become Emory's second president. Longstreet's name was better known than the college itself, which was an outgrowth of the Georgia Conference Manual Labor School.

Manual labor schools were an educational fad of the 1830s suggested by Philipp Emmanueal von Feilenberg, an associate of Johann Henrich Pestalozzi, who established such a plan at Hofwyl in Germany in 1805. Ignatius Few, who had read von Feilenberg's and Pestalozzi's theories, was the director of the school, and he later became Emory's first president when the manual labor school and part of its physical plant were incorporated into a college. The manual labor concept was attractive to Longstreet, who always believed in plain living and hard work, and he tried to instill in his students some of his own enthusiasm.

In his inaugural address, which he delivered on 10 February 1840, he stressed the essentially Christian nature of the study-labor program at Emory. He referred to Emory as an "infant seminary" and noted that the college's basic textbook in morals would be the Bible and that all lessons in physics would "begin and end with its Author." Consistent with the spirit of *Georgia Scenes* and later of *William Mitten* was the new president's assertion that "the guardianship of youth . . . [is] the most important, honorable, and sacred trust that can be confided to man." Tactfully, the new leader deprecated his own intellectual abilities and complimented the faculty on their experience and wisdom. The students he implored "to unite mental and manual labor in indissoluble bonds, and to consecrate the union with spotless robes of piety." Later he warned that America's besetting sin was the "idolatry of wealth" and urged them to make Emory an oasis of more wholesome and basic values.[29]

No administrative endorsement could increase the efficiency of student labor, however, nor counter the resistance of these young Georgians to such a program, which required constant supervision and heavy outlays of capital and equipment. A document appointing Longstreet as attorney for the Georgia Manual Labor School is preserved in the Emory University archives. Dated 12 September 1843, it attests to the duties he might have to perform related to suits and settlements touching the school. Shortly after this document was signed, the whole student labor program was abandoned as being unworkable.

The new college administrator was plagued with budgetary problems; he cut salaries, abolished scholarships, and reduced the staff. In addition, the college was forced to sell land in order to meet its expenses, as shown in a deed notarized by Longstreet on 26 March 1842. A parcel of land, consisting of several lots covering approximately 106 acres, was sold by the trustees of the college to the Georgian entrepreneur Alexander Mans for $1,790; an interesting stipulation attached to the deed reads "that if the said Alexander Mans, his heirs, executors, administrators and assigns shall at any time hereafter sell or allow to be sold any intoxicating liquors on said land, or shall play or allow to be played there on any games of chance then this conveyance to be void and the lot or parcel of land herein conveyed to be forfeited and to become the property of said trustees."[30] Such a measure to ensure that property next to the college not be used in ways that might corrupt the students' morals possibly reflected the new president's concern for his young charges, as well as his temperance beliefs. This stipulation naturally displeased the students and local merchants. They also objected to Longstreet's tight-fisted attitudes toward money, for few people realized the president often dipped into personal capital to meet the institution's commitments. Although under Longstreet's administration Emory's student body increased to rival that of the state university, he was unable to improve the physical plant or the endowment fund.

Judson Ward has commented on the mixed frustrations and achievements of the Judge's tenure:

His administration was not so brilliant as might have been anticipated. Still he managed the internal affairs so that the student conduct was notably good, and he succeeded in building firmly on the educational foundations [Ignatius] Few had laid. When he resigned in 1848 there was less doubt about the permanency of the institution, and the reputation of the college had been extended to a much wider circle.[31]

Although his administration was only moderately successful, Longstreet's personal life during the Emory years seems to have been unusually happy. His nephew James, later to become the famous Civil War general, often visited the Longstreets at the college. As the boy's educational guardian, Longstreet, who had counseled so many of the sons of friends and colleagues in his various professional capacities, had an opportunity to exert his influence in a more intimate way.

In Mrs. James Longstreet's biography of her husband many years later, she notes that, like his uncle at the same age, James was "mischievous, full of fun and frolic."[32] Glenn Tucker believes that early contact between uncle and nephew was a crucial factor in James's development: "To the remarkable Augustus must be attributed a share in the general's staunch qualities— his integrity, his ambition, and perhaps even his striking writing ability, which distinguished him among the top Confederates." Young James also emulated the manner and deportment of his uncle, sensing his "magnetic presence," which according to Tucker the future general "seems to have caught during their association as preceptor and pupil."[33] Specifically, Longstreet shaped his nephew's career by arranging with the help of his friends McDuffie and Calhoun for James's appointment to West Point, a plan discussed with his brother before the latter's death. Frances Longstreet, for her part, probably enjoyed looking after an attractive young man who reminded her of their own lost son.

Other young men besides his nephew were influenced by the Judge. One of the most talented, L. Q. C. Lamar, was a frequent guest in the president's mansion and was destined to become, first, his great admirer and protégé and within the decade, his son-in-law. The Longstreet family provided Lamar's first contact with "famous" people since by this time the whole Emory community was aware of the growing reputation of *Georgia Scenes* along the east coast as far as New England. Not surprisingly, at ceremonial occasions, such an author and educator was much in demand, and when his old headmaster, Dr. Moses Waddel, died, Longstreet was naturally called back to the academy to eulogize him.

Whatever his youthful perceptions of Headmaster Waddel may have been, Longstreet in later years believed he had been his principal intellectual and spiritual tutor. He assumed Waddel's posture as the moral guide of youth, and his own role as an educator confirmed his strong identification with the teacher he had revered as a boy and the mentor he had followed during his adolescent years. He maintained friendships with various members of the Waddel family, growing nostalgic and teary-eyed at any mention of the old academy. This sentimental tendency in their college president endeared him to the students and faculty at Emory. However, they found his frequently auto-cratic treatment of them less appealing. Once Longstreet had made an immediate, conclusive judgment, he was intractable. When he stipulated restrictions on land sales near the school or enforced unpopular aspects of the work program, he refused to listen to any discontented voices from the college community. Outside the campus he was equally outspoken and authoritative so that in his presence no one dared challenge the validity of the Gospels, the wisdom of the temperance movement, or the moral legitimacy of slavery. His convictions on this outmoded institution, in particular, were infrangible. He was very fond of Negroes when they were content with a subservient position but wrathful if they aspired to equality. Northerners who accepted the existence of slavery were decent people, but abolitionists were Satan's henchmen.

Division in the Church and the Slavery Issue

Therefore, it is not surprising that when he went to New York in May 1844 to attend the General Conference of the Methodist church, he expected to find his fellow Methodists, North and South, in accord with his own views on slavery. Granted, there had not been much significant division in the church over the slavery question in the past because Methodism was strongest in the South and able to shape church policy. A decade before Longstreet's birth, some northern Methodists made slavery a divisive issue, but within a few years the controversy abated. When Longstreet entered the church in his middle years, the institution of slavery was generally accepted by Methodists in all parts of the country. Soon afterward, however, there were rumblings in the northern parishes followed by theological debates. Proslavery forces interpreted Paul's Epistle to Timothy as a condonation of slavery. The antislavery faction emphasized that a slave owner could not truly be awakened to Christ.[34] In March 1843, a number of dissidents opposed to the church's laissez-faire attitude toward slavery founded a new denomination, the Wesleyan Methodist church. Conservatives in the old church were glad to be rid of the Wesleyan group and anticipated no further trouble.

As soon as Longstreet arrived in New York, however, he

discovered that his old friend, Bishop Andrew of Georgia, was under attack for owning slaves. The convention began with Longstreet and the Georgians defending Andrew, and the New England clergy presenting a series of antislavery resolutions. By June the Methodist church was divided into slave-holding and non-holding branches. Bishop William Capers, a trustee of Emory like Bishop Andrew, had proposed such a motion on the third of June, and Longstreet had followed it two days later with a statement that abolitionist Methodists had no control over the southern churches. From that moment Longstreet refused to trust a northern Methodist, and thus almost two decades before the Civil War, he and other religious and educational leaders were forced to recognize the dramatic increase of tensions that were threatening the Union.

When Longstreet had returned to Georgia after the church divided, he wrote a letter to the ecclesiastical publication the *New York Advocate and Journal,* explaining his feelings about the recent conflict within the church. He was enraged when the editors refused to publish what they considered a highly personal attack. The *Southern Christian Advocate* in Charleston was naturally more obliging, and it printed three of Longstreet's letters, each a biblical defense of slavery. In one the Judge insisted that "abolition among churchmen is a mania, a fanatical monster." The author's old instinct for politics had resurfaced and merged with his religious zeal. For the next twenty years this powerful combination of political and religious passion would dominate his life. Other intelligent leaders in his region also subordinated their personal and political concerns to an impassioned, moralistic defense of slavery and of the southern way of life.

These letters are probably the ones Longstreet refers to in a message dated 24 February 1845 to Dr. T. E. Bond of New York, an editor of the *New York Advocate and Journal.* Bond's role in this affair and his attitude toward Longstreet are unknown. Possibly he felt obliged to report the southern view of the conference once tempers on both sides had cooled down. In any event, he seems to have written Longstreet first, soliciting the latter's angry response. After he offers personal reasons for not writing sooner to Bond, he asks why his letters have not been published:

Before I left Texas I wrote out the three numbers which you have upon Paul's letter to Philemon, and three more which have never been sent to you; for I instructed my wife to send on to you a number *weekly,* until I reach the third number, and if at that time she saw no notice of them in the Advocate & Journal to withhold the rest. She did so. In the last number I beg the four gentlemen addressed to consider themselves called on for a reply in the order of their names. This of course would remove one of your difficulties about publishing them (the likelihood of all wishing to reply at once) but the essay being twice as long as you suppose it to be would of course double the embarrassment which you feel at devoting so much of your paper to this controversy. As to the position in which I place the gentlemen addressed, I do not know that I do them injustice, but this might be easily rectified by substituting "the position" for "your position." If they do not think it *sinful* in a Christian Minister to hold slaves I wish them to say so in the face of the world. It is a prevalent opinion at the north that a slaveholder cannot be a Christian, and this opinion gains strength from the manner in which northern Christians of a different opinion treat the subject. They do not oppose the erroneous opinion, they vote to displace a minister that holds slaves, and they one and all I believe consider slavery a great "moral evil." This last term is used upon all occasions without qualification or explanation so far as I know, and hence the opinion is every day gaining ground that slavery is "a crying sin." Dr. Durbin, on the conference floor, seemed to be shocked at the idea of this addressing scripture to support slavery; though he did not trouble himself much to meet the Scriptures quoted upon him. It was with great reluctance that I sought a place in the columns of the Advocate & Journal for my very voluminous remarks from Paul to Philemon, but I supposed the importance of the subject might excuse their prolixity to your readers. Still I am willing to abide your judgment and if with these explanations, you feel that it is best not to publish them in your paper, I submit without a murmur to the exclusion of them from your columns.[35]

Whatever Bond's personal response to this testy note, the *Advocate and Journal* appears not to have found Longstreet's treatises suitable for publication. Such treatises were all extravagantly phrased, more likely to provoke shock and dismay than productive discussion.

Longstreet spent the next year touring Methodist churches in the South and establishing the separateness of that institution from the northern branch. Professing that he hoped to avoid a serious confrontation between the two regions, he seemed unaware of the psychological impact of ecclesiastical secession on the stability of the nation.

At a meeting in Louisville Longstreet helped forge the identity of the new Southern Methodist church. Supporting Longstreet's ecclesiastical views, H. D. Bascomb of Kentucky wrote a book called *Methodism and Slavery,* which John C. Calhoun and Henry Clay endorsed. It was harshly reviewed by the northern Methodist, Rev. Dr. Peck, in a pamphlet called *Slavery and the Episcopacy.* Longstreet, angered by Peck's review of Bascomb's book and frustrated that his own views could not be known to northern readers, nevertheless determined that all the South would learn them. He wrote a pamphlet consisting of five letters addressed to Dr. Peck and three other clergymen who had led the opposition at the Methodist conference. He called his pamphlet *Letters on the Epistle of Paul to Philemon or the Connection of Apostolical Christianity with Slavery.* All of the letters attempt to prove that slavery was an institution that was not sinful and that biblical evidence of its evils must be produced "without taking recourse to the Declaration of Independence or throwing up a breastwork out of the long-forsaken rubbish of the social contract." The wide acceptance of Longstreet's pamphlet in the South was gratifying to its author, but he still longed to convert the North to his point of view.

A Voice from the South

Longstreet's friend Thompson, at this time editor of the Baltimore-based *Western Continent,* agreed to publish another series of proslavery letters. The recipient of the Judge's wrath on this occasion would be the state of Massachusetts which he considered the "ringleader" of the abolitionist movement. Possibly he imagined that Massachusetts' competitive neighbors, such as Connecticut and Rhode Island, might be more sympathetic to his ideas. The letters, collected in pamphlet form, were published by the West Continent Press in 1847 under the title *A Voice from the South: Letters from Georgia to Massachusetts.*

Even Longstreet's lengthy subtitle stressed his scholarly intention:

Containing an article from the Charleston *Mercury* on the Wilmot Proviso, together with the 4th article of the Constitution, the law of Congress, the Nullification law of Pennsylvania, the Resolution of Ten of the Free States, the Resolution of Virginia, Georgia and Alabama, and Mr. Calhoun's resolution on the Senate of the United States.

A Voice from the South is a somewhat better argued document than the *Letters on the Epistle of Paul to Philemon,* which grew out of the Judge's impotent rage following the church's General Conference. The unacceptability of Longstreet's racial attitudes to the modern reader makes it difficult to appreciate his skill in constructing an effective piece of social and political propaganda. He begins his letters by addressing the home of abolitionism as "Dear Sister Mass." but by the fourth letter has simplified his salutation to a rather curt "Madam." His key legal point is that Congress has no jurisdiction over the holding of slaves. He then attempts to isolate Massachusetts from other New England states, calling her "the chief agent" of a personal attack on Georgia.

In the first letter, Longstreet plays on the guilt of the northern reader by suggesting that it was Yankee ships that brought the slaves and "abandoned them half-dying." He also delivers the first of many unspecified threats: *"The result of your movements will be more disastrous to you and your allies than to me and mine"* (italics are Longstreet's). In his second letter, the author maligns the Yankee character, calling it "too forward, too tricky, too covetous." He refers to the burning of Catholic churches by the Puritans and their refusal to support the goals of the French Revolution. The third letter asserts that freeing slaves would be irresponsible, since the North does not want them. By the fifth letter, Longstreet poses as the strict constitutionalist who is trying to prevent Massachusetts from subverting American democracy's basic document. He saves his strongest volley for the sixth letter in which he reminds New Englanders of their early persecution of dissidents, noting, "You have driven from your churches as good men as this land, if not this world, holds." He may have observed at Yale, years before, a masochistic tendency in some Yankees to bemoan their ancestors' misdeeds.

A Voice from the South also contains letters from Georgia to the southern states, asking for support, arguing that Massachu-

setts "may turn the government into a machine, that shall work
as a screw upon the South, and as a mint to the North," and
concluding that the author's motives are "as pure as anything
emanated from Georgia." Appearing in eight editions by 1849,
Longstreet's pamphlet was extremely successful in the South,
where it conformed to the prejudices of the majority. It is doubtful, however, that it was ever read by more than a handful of
northerners. During that same year, Longstreet conducted Atlanta's first
religious revival with his friend Bishop Andrews. Together they
urged Georgians to restructure their lives by renewing their
faith in the Gospels. Although the revival resembled a political
rally at times, especially when Paul's Epistles were cited, the
college president and the bishop, along with their congregation,
convinced themselves that God's purposes had been well served
by their crusade.

Longstreet's Increased Political Involvement

While Longstreet was writing in general terms of the southern
slaveholder's antipathy toward abolitionists in *A Voice from the
South* and joining in evangelical religious meetings, he was also
actively involved in specific political decisions in his region.
The states' rights issue had been a major rallying point in every
national election for two decades. Longstreet and other prominent southerners carefully scrutinized the platforms of presidential and vice-presidential candidates on the issues of sovereignty,
tariffs, and slavery. During the twelve years from 1832 to 1844
in which Calhoun served as senator, Longstreet believed, quite
realistically, that a political philosophy compatible with his own
was being aggressively maintained. In 1844 Calhoun accepted
a position in President John Tyler's cabinet as secretary of state.
Here he hoped to expedite the admission of Texas into the
union as a slaveholding state, thereby garnering more support
for the southern cause. His opponents, led by Pennsylvanian
David Wilmot from the U. S. House of Representatives, sponsored the Wilmot Proviso in 1846, stipulating that newly acquired territory should be closed to slavery. Although it passed
in the House twice, the proviso was defeated both times in
the Senate. One unexpected ally of those who opposed the

amendment was Lewis Cass, a Democrat, who had been the governor of the Michigan Frontier from 1813 to 1831 and then served as secretary of war under President Jackson. New Hampshire–born Cass was a strong union man, who had supported Jackson's first tariff bill and had joined him in opposing the Nullification Ordinance. In 1848 he surprised his party by writing a letter to a political colleague explaining that the Wilmot Proviso was in opposition to his own notion of popular sovereignty, his theory that the people of a territory must decide the slavery issue for themselves.

Longstreet immediately saw the advantages of aligning the South behind Cass in the next presidential election. As a former western governor, Cass could create a western and southern coalition that might defeat the North on the states' rights issue. Therefore Longstreet, with missionary zeal, sought to enlist the politically powerful Calhoun as a supporter of Cass. With his usual sense of drama, Longstreet drafted a letter to Calhoun on the Fourth of July, 1848, urging him to rally behind Cass and offering to stand with him against the abolitionists:

Van Buren is forming a party upon the sole principle of the Wilmot Provision. This party as Van very plainly sees will overpower any party which opposes it at the North. Cass with a strong party at his back is out in direct opposition to the Proviso. At last then we have a party which will carry our arguments upon this head to the doors of the Northern people and whose political salvation is stacked upon them. Now suppose the South in mass rallies to this party and elects Cass, what must be the consequence? That party is forever detached from the abolition and the far West might unite with it. It will grow stronger and stronger; for there is no sympathy between the east and the west. The only reason why the west is not with us now to a man, is, that it had no interest in the South, and would not uselessly hazard any thing in vindicating their rights. The Southwest will be every day growing stronger and inspiring confidence in our Northern auxiliaries. These powers united will in eight years' time from the 4 March next campaign abolitioning in to its merited contempt. Let Cass be by the vote of the South elected and we shall have candidates enough at the North who will be ready to give any pledges that the South may demand upon the subject of Slavery. And this they may do without any compromise of principle. In fact *principle* demands that they should do this now and most of them know it; but hitherto

they have been awed into delay and inactivity by the abolition clamor
which they could gain some by opposing. "But is Cass reliable? I
know more about him than you do." I answer "Yes, perfectly reliable,
if for no better reason than that his interest and that of his partner
leave him no alternative but to do right." This pledge is given upon
the delicate question and it is a rare thing that a man made President
upon a principle, abandon it during his term of office and what Cass
may do when he gets out of office is of but little consequence. But
I have no fears of him out of office. I should not fear Van Buren or
Tom Corwen in his situation. Withal all life is uncertain. Suppose
Cass should die Butler is our President, a much safer man than Taylor
and he will strengthen the Union with our Northern friends. Never
have I seen since the birth of abolitionism a time so favorable to a
final and complete triumph of the South as the present; but to avail
herself of it, she must renounce all claims upon the Presidency for
two terms at least. After that she will probably alternate with the
North and West. Set me down as no prophet if every word of this
does prove true; and verily if all my prophecies had been recorded
and remembered they would reflect no little credit upon my forecast.

Let us now look at the other side of the picture. Suppose we support
Taylor [Zachary Taylor, U. S. President, 1849–50] and elect him.
He will give up perfect security upon the slavery question for four
years and thus friendless at the North and Impotent at the South.
The whole Northern power comes down upon us without mercy and
without a disguise for injustice and oppression. I hardly think the
union will endure four years afterwards. Suppose Taylor should die;
where then are we? Withal who knows any thing about General Taylor.
I dread any man who comes into power under a Whig nomination.
Harrison wasn't anything until he was elected; and then he was just
a mass of wax in Clay's hands.[36]

An experienced politician like Calhoun must already have
been sensitive to the implications of possible western support
of Cass and the new popular sovereignty movement, but his
feelings toward Cass as a person were clearly ambivalent. Cass
and Martin Van Buren, who began his political career as a Democratic senator from New York, were the same age as Calhoun
and fellow party members during the Jackson administration.
Serious ideological differences in the early 1830s had caused
the two northern-born politicians to side with Jackson against
Calhoun on the nullification issue. Furthermore, Van Buren had
taken advantage of the Peggy O'Neale affair to purge the Jack-

son administration of Calhoun supporters.[37] Calhoun never forgave Van Buren and shortly afterward blocked the latter's confirmation as minister to England in the Senate.

Cass was more a behind-the-scenes man than Van Buren, but he sided with Jackson and Van Buren on both the political and the social issues. He was rewarded by being made Jackson's secretary of war for five years, a post held by Calhoun under President Monroe, and by being appointed minister to France by both Jackson and Van Buren.

Thus, Calhoun may have smiled wryly over Longstreet's rhetorical question, "But is Cass reliable?" and his answer, "Yes . . . his interest and that of his party leave him no alternative but to do right." It is impossible to know if Longstreet's letter helped to influence Calhoun's acceptance of Cass or if he had already considered supporting his old colleague. An experienced politician quickly learns to bury old grudges when expediency demands it. In any event, divisiveness weakened the Democrats so that Zachary Taylor, whom Longstreet and Calhoun dreaded, was elected president. What is significant is that Longstreet had once again turned to Calhoun as the ultimate defender of southern principles in his growing alarm over violations of what he called "the constitutional rights of slave-holders." Although publicly he was frustrated by the northern attitudes toward the South and its institutions, privately, at least, he enjoyed in his family relations the peace and harmony that eluded him elsewhere.

Still in his forties, Longstreet was now nationally recognized as an author. Georgians were proud of his writings although they knew him best as an incorruptible judge, a stalwart defender of the southern Methodist church, and an idealistic college president.

Departure from Emory

The tranquility of his life was soon interrupted by rumors that he was being considered for the presidency of the University of Mississippi. In his eagerness to prove himself available for the job, he resigned from Emory only to discover that the trustees at Mississippi had elected another man as president. Deeply chagrined, Longstreet refused to accept retirement peaceably; instead, he agreed to become president of Centenary College in Louisiana, one of a number of small sectarian institutions, which was more than willing to be led by a man of Longstreet's reputation. Selected in haste, Centenary was an unfortunate choice, and the Longstreets regretted the time they spent there. The school was provincial, the students unruly, and the faculty undistinguished. The only serendipitous outcome of the Centenary year was Longstreet's brief return to writing, which became at once his defense against unhappiness and his vengeance on a community he despised; for *William Mitten,* his novel of spoiled and corrupted youth, originated in the despair of his Louisiana exile. Writing could only ease, not eradicate, his frustration over his exile, however, and unable to face the prospect of another year at Centenary, he resigned his office at commencement and made plans to return to Georgia. Before his departure he unexpectedly learned that he had been elected president of the University of Mississippi at Oxford to replace George Holmes whom the board of trustees had earlier chosen in place of Longstreet. Longstreet accepted the position by mail but returned nevertheless to Georgia where John Waddel had traveled to bring him the good news in person. Happy that Waddel's faith in him had been vindicated, Longstreet pretended surprise at the announcement. Certainly he was pleased to have what was considered a very prestigious appointment, but his assuaged pride was one of his few consolations in the fall semester of 1849.

When he arrived in Mississippi, he found the student body to be even more unruly and disorganized than it had been at Centenary. Holmes had been a completely inadequate administrator and had virtually abandoned his post the previous April. This situation proved politically advantageous for Longstreet. Because the trustees were embarrassed that they had not chosen him in the first place, they were prepared to be extremely cooperative with their new leader. Besides, the state of the university had reached a point where almost any administrative change would constitute an improvement. Edward Mayes, in discussing the history of education in Mississippi, attests that "very rarely, if ever, was an institution attended by a body of students so disorderly and turbulent."[38] It is worth noting that this "large" and important southern university had an enrollment at this time of only 76 students. Five years after Longstreet had assumed office, the number of students had risen to 225.

Wade does not make clear how Longstreet was able to restore order to the university except in suggesting that he had natural persuasive ability, tact when necessary, and the full cooperation of his faculty. It may have been that the new president's passion for order and discipline was an almost welcome change after the chaos of the years preceding his installation. After six years at Oxford, Longstreet evidently felt secure enough about his position to press the state of Mississippi for $900,000 promised to the university. Although only a portion of this money actually found its way into university coffers, the growing power of the university and its chief administrator was illustrated by the boldness of the request. Some insight into Longstreet's university presence is evident, too, in his personal life. After making each major step of his academic career, he was able to persuade his family, including his daughters and their families, to uproot themselves and follow him. Longstreet's sons-in-law claimed fondness for the old gentleman, and he usually saw to it that they were provided with good jobs in each community. He also maintained close ties with his nephew James.

A letter addressed by James to "My Dear Doctor" and dated 3 May 1854, reflects the nephew's dependence on his uncle in financial affairs. He writes: "When you receive the money I wish that you would send Louise a New York or Washington draft for three hundred dollars, and send the rest either in Mobile or New Orleans or New York drafts to William D. Longstreet." Then he adds a geographical comment which would appeal to his uncle's wide interests in his nation: "An officer passed through here a few days ago who has just made the trip from San Diego to San Antonio in sixty-one days. He found a little shorter route than Cooke's wagon route." In closing, James affectionately remarks, "Write me whenever you have leisure," adding, perhaps playfully, "give my best love to all and a farewell kiss to Mary Anne, that she cheated me out of the day I left you."[39] That James would write such a light-hearted postscript suggests that the stern judge had his gentler moments and that, moreover, he was closely and benevolently involved in his nephew's affairs. In a letter Longstreet had written on 1 February 1851, he requested that John McPherson Berrien appoint James as lieutenant colonel or major of one of two new regiments being raised by Congress; a postscript suggested that he "pass this letter to my friends Dawson, Cobb, Toombs, Ste-

phens—in short all the Georgia Delegation Genl. Foote and
J. Thompson of this State, and beg them to consider it addressed
to them, as well as to yourself."[40] Longstreet would not seek
special favors for himself, but he would never hesitate to ensure
the welfare of his family and friends. Clearly, he had in abun-
dance that special mixture of self-assurance, ambition, and style
that characterizes effective authority figures.

Involvement in his nephew's career and in the activities of
his daughters' families occupied much of Longstreet's spare time
in Mississippi but could not altogether compensate him for once
again being confined in a provincial outpost. Wade notes that
even in 1850 Oxford was too small to be listed by the census
takers. What pleasures could a tiny village have offered a restless,
ambitious man like Longstreet?

The president of a small college in the nineteenth century
usually had teaching as well as administrative duties. Longstreet
taught moral philosophy, rhetoric, religious, and even political
economy courses. He arranged for a position for his son-in-
law, Lamar, in the mathematics department. But his true interests
did not lie in the classroom or in the president's office, and
he soon became fascinated with the money-making opportunities
of real estate speculation. Eventually, most of his time was involved in buying or selling land and his impulse to enact business
transactions became so obsessive that his old friends in Georgia
began to complain that he never answered their letters. He
shirked both his teaching and administrative duties. When the
trustees and some students grumbled about his negligence, he
offered testily to resign, but one cynical observer noted that
Longstreet's willingness to step down could not be sincere, since
he was "making money too fast for him to be reduced to
resign."[41]

The President and the Know Nothings

Along with his business interests, Longstreet kept a hand in
Mississippi state politics, although he was scornful of the futile
attempts of the Whig party to expand its base by the growth
of the Know Nothing party in Mississippi. The Whigs had refused to take a sufficiently strong stand on the slavery issue to
suit most southern conservatives, and the party fell into disarray.

In Georgia, for example, it had almost disappeared by 1855.[42] Some former Whigs defected to the Democratic party but many were attracted to the Know Nothings. Officially known as the American party, the Know Nothings began in New York City in 1849 under the banner of nativism. That is, their members were composed largely of Anglo-American stock who resented the migration of Germans to the Middle West and the growing power of Irish and Italian Catholics in New York, and they acquired the name "Know Nothings" because they necessarily had to cloak their bigotry and spread their doctrines in a kind of fraternal secrecy. Royce C. McCrary has recently argued that the Know Nothings hoped to develop a strong Unionist party.[43]

In Georgia their only distinguished member was Benjamin H. Hill of LaGrange. At one time, John McPherson Berrien was rumored to be a Know Nothing candidate, but he died before he could make an impact on the party. Longstreet probably distrusted the movement for two reasons: first, he was too much of a states' rights man to entertain notions of unionism; second, his friendship with the Roman Catholic cleric, Bishop John Barry, made the strong anti-Catholic bias of the American party distasteful to him. He therefore availed himself of every opportunity to denounce the movement and its supporters. Many Mississippians believed it was undignified and even unethical for him to use his position at the university as a platform for political views. The Reverend William Winans of Natchez soon assailed Longstreet in the Natchez *Courier* for his attitude toward the Know Nothings. The Judge had loved a good newspaper article debate ever since the days when he himself was a small-time editor; he wrote a reply to Reverend Winans called *Know Nothingism Unveiled,* and it was published by the Congressional *Globe* in 1855.

Only eight pages long, the article is nevertheless a good example of Longstreet's undiminished fighting spirit in his later years. In it he stated that only a fool would attempt to change a man's religion through harassment. And he added that once "the work of crushing churches is begun in this country, it is not going to stop with the overthrow of one."[44] Ironically, considering his own theological defense of slavery, he lamented the mixture of politics and religion in the Know Nothing platform. He held that his main grievance against the party was its continued ties with the northern branch of the Methodist church, which he claimed drove away the southern branch, "blistered them by calumny, and pocketed all the partnership funds." Longstreet here and elsewhere identified the Know Nothings in the South with abolitionists in the North, and, as has been noted, he could never forgive the northern church for its position in the slavery issue. Ending with a denunciation of secret Know Nothing practices, Longstreet suggested that their persecution of the Catholics could serve only to strengthen the Roman church. His position here recalls his attack on Yankee religious prejudice in *A Voice from the South,* for he was eager that his own region should not be blamed for attitudes he had once criticized in the North.

Trouble with the Trustees

Longstreet's involvement with the Know Nothing controversy, combined with his reputation for being a major real estate speculator in the Oxford area, made him increasingly unpopular with the University of Mississippi's trustees. Furthermore, the Democratic party counted heavily on Longstreet's report and had distributed campaign material called "The Letters of President Longstreet." The use of his office for propaganda purposes struck his opponents as unseemly. Recognizing that he was the center of a controversy, Longstreet offered his resignation to the university, possibly hoping that he would thereby provoke declarations of renewed loyalty. The trustees asked him to withdraw his resignation and conferred on him a Doctor of Divinity degree, but he considered this gesture insufficient proof of their sincerity. He was rich now and did not depend on his $2,500-a-year salary. In addition, he had already received an honorary degree from Yale. Dramatically, he tendered his resignation once again and it was, to his amazement, accepted; perhaps he had outmaneuvered himself, for he did not appear prepared for retirement. To add to his frustration, he was crushed that his own chosen successor, John Waddel, was passed over in favor of a New England professor, Frederick A. P. Barnard, destined later to be president of Columbia College in New York.

Despondent that his influence had come to an end, Longstreet moved to a small plantation in Abbeville, Mississippi, where he was joined by his daughters and sons-in-law, the Lamars and the Branhams, who urged him to forget the petty grievances of his Oxford years and to enjoy retirement. In times of trouble his strong family ties were a great source of comfort. In 1857 he was appointed an honorary member of the Smithsonian Institution, but Wade declares that "the position meant little to him"[45] although it must have been gratifying for him to know that he still had a nationwide reputation.

Soon more evidence of his continued fame arrived. The trustees at the University of South Carolina asked him to become president of that institution and he accepted. Coyly he had first asked Mrs. Longstreet to make the decision, but she wisely refused, knowing by now that when her husband was offered a chance for additional power and prestige, his acceptance of the challenge was inevitable.

A New Home and a Novel

Although they were accustomed to life in college towns, the Longstreet family, moving to South Carolina in 1858, found Columbia to be a decidedly more established and affluent community than its counterparts in Georgia, Louisiana, or Mississippi, as this contemporary account of life in Columbia, which appeared in the September 1860 issue of *DeBow's Review,* confirms:

Columbia, which is, or may be called the Garden city is one of the choicest spots in the South for a family residence. It is perfectly healthy at all seasons of the year, has good water, most excellent schools, and a very advanced, refined and wealthy society. During the sessions of the legislature, it is the centre of the liveliest interest, and balls, parties and the most charming social intercourse prevail. The town is well laid out. The streets are wide, and attached to nearly every house is a garden of some sort, and many have gardens, which, in extent and variety and beauty, are not surpassed anywhere.[46]

To the citizens of Columbia, Longstreet's former academic appointments seemed insignificant—they were missionary outposts in a crude frontier. The nearly two hundred students at the university were more sophisticated, and many had read or discussed *Georgia Scenes* in preparation for their new leader's tenure. They found it rowdy and coarse by the standards of their own time and eagerly anticipated a boisterous maverick who would bring some fun to a staid community. But twenty-five years of wielding power had transformed the author. Student expectations of discovering a good-hearted, provincial eccentric, a casual teacher-friend whom they could nickname "Ned Brace," were quickly disabused. Longstreet seemed older perhaps than they had imagined, formidable, a stranger to the mentality that had shaped his first humorous sketches. As a teacher he was ineffective and tedious; he fared somewhat better as an administrator, but many of his problems stemmed from the students' disappointment at their new president's behavior. One day, taking a cue from "The Turn Out," they decided to bar all teachers from the college campus. It is doubtful that the elderly administrator ever saw the relationship between his earlier story and the disciplinary crisis he confronted. Taking a firm stand, he expelled those students involved in the incident although some were later readmitted after completing arduous academic tasks. The student body as a whole resigned itself to an uninspired administration, and order and discipline were finally established at the university.

Longstreet could never reconcile himself to the South Carolinians' want of industry and preoccupation with pleasure, particularly drinking and gambling. Nevertheless, the Longstreet household adapted to its new environment, for although the Judge's frugality was challenged by the relatively high cost of living in Columbia, his sense of dignity demanded that he and his wife not fall behind the rest of the community in maintaining a proper social posture. Charles Hutson writing for the *Sewanee Review* in July 1910, recalls some of the splendor of the Longstreet presidency at Carolina, and Wade has paraphrased his article:

There was a fine house for the President to live in, and there were countless invitations for the President to participate in all manner of social activities. Fine horses were in the stables. . . . Fine curtains were hanging in the parlor windows, curtains made originally for President Buchanan, in Germany, to go in the White House, but refused by him on account of their costliness.[47]

In this opulent setting, Longstreet may have recalled his tirades against affected or extravagant society in *Georgia Scenes*. Once he had thought the young students at Centenary College were spoiled and worthless, but they seemed stoic in comparison to the planters' sons who drifted aimlessly about Columbia. It is ironic that Longstreet's caveat against indulging children and particularly against the perils of drink and gambling should finally be published when he was firmly ensconced in just such an atmosphere.

The judge's novel, *William Mitten: or a Youth of Brilliant Talents Who Was Ruined by Bad Luck,* was published serially in a new weekly periodical, *Southern Field and Fireside,* between 28 May and 19 November of 1859; five years later it was printed as a book in Macon, Georgia. His new book as well as his position at the university made Longstreet a celebrity in the new community and he and his wife were frequently entertained. In their elegantly furnished house the Longstreets enjoyed a more sophisticated social life than any Mississippi town could have provided in that era. When students or faculty came by to call, the Judge might entertain them with his glass flute; at other times, he would be crochety or vague, common failings of an old man. But the prosperous and often pampered offspring of Carolina planters were not easily intimidated by authority figures nor easily dissuaded from Rabelaisian pursuits. Most of South Carolina's students were affluent young aristocrats with regional pride, which Longstreet admired, but without professional goals, which he deplored. One has the impression that Longstreet was never fully in control at South Carolina. Perhaps to compensate for his uninspired leadership, he attempted to show his impartiality in pedagogical matters. Addressing the trustees on 9 May 1859, he explained that he had replaced quality textbooks for an outmoded textbook in a political economy course without regard to the more competent author's views of slavery:

> The latter [textbook] is infinitely preferable as a textbook to the former. It emanated to be sure from an abolitionist; but there is not a word in it upon the subject of slavery, nothing sectional.[48]

Then on 30 November of the same year he seized the opportunity to praise Harvard's science program, suggesting it might become a model for South Carolina students. Considering his extreme distrust of the state of Massachusetts, the trustees must have wondered at his praise of the industriousness of New England students:

There is a scientific department in Harvard University corresponding very nearly with that proposed for this institution. That is the oldest college in the Union, has long occupied first position among the colleges of the country; several of the professors have a world-wide reputation; it is situated near the third city in the Union in point of population; in a densely populated state, whose youth seek education for a living rather than its enjoyment.[49]

There is no evidence to indicate that the president's attempts at curriculum reform were any more successful than his efforts to enforce discipline.

Longstreet and Secessionism

Nevertheless, the austere president who had first been such a disappointment to his students finally captured their imagination with what appears, retrospectively, to have been a mutually destructive obsession. The South Carolina students were not scholarly and needed a cause to occupy their energies apart from drinking and gambling; Longstreet longed for an audience, an adoring youthful crowd who admired his leadership, and the issue that brought the leader and potential followers together was, of course, secession. As early as 1857 in his baccalaureate address, Longstreet had alarmed the trustees, including his old friend J. L. Petigru, with his extravagant threats to the North.[50] A display of enmity for the North, in particular Massachusetts, was the one banner under which his unruly students would march, along with the doctrine of white supremacy threatened by the abolitionists. Not surprisingly, the boys' parents, by and large reactionary plantation owners, supported their heated political sentiments. Longstreet correctly assessed the mood of the campus to be increasingly hostile to the Union.

Fortified by this support, he left for England in the summer of 1860 to attend the International Statistical Congress. Howell Cobb, then the secretary of the treasury, had commissioned

Longstreet to take part in the conference. The latter may have hoped to win the sympathy of the British for the problems of the American South, or at least he may have considered it his responsibility to defend slavery should the issue arise in formal or informal discussions at the meeting. It is doubtful that he appreciated the beauty of London or the cultural opportunities it afforded, because all his energy, intelligence, and passions were involved in his obsessive desire to vindicate the southern view of slavery. Lingering frustrations over the quiet failure of *William Mitten,* his declining physical strength as he approached his seventieth year, and his increasing inability to cope with teaching and administrative duties were all sublimated in his general rage at the Union. He was cantankerous, hypersensitive, and sometimes irrational; in such a volatile state of mind, he approached the other delegates to the conference warily. He was defensively effusive in his expressions of affection for America and psychologically attuned to vent his feelings in some dramatic way. He may have resented the relative insignificance of his position in an international arena. All the delegates clamored for a glimpse of Prince Albert when he addressed the conference; in Columbia, Longstreet himself was the celebrity, the grand old man of the community.

The Judge did not wait long to play his major scene. Shortly after Prince Albert's speech, a senile and patronizing English peer, Lord Brougham, drew public attention to the presence of a Negro delegate, the American-born M. F. Delaney, then a Canadian citizen. Delaney was courteously applauded, and Longstreet boiled over with rage. He believed Brougham had deliberately introduced Delaney's name as a means of embarrassing the American delegation; he was probably distressed as well by seeing such respectful behavior toward a black man. For these and other reasons that will probably never be known, Longstreet withdrew from the conference. The British and American newspapers carried an account of the incident, but it is unlikely that the Judge's exit was the *coup de théâtre* which he had intended. He cut short what was to have been a long European vacation and came home, vowing never to return to Europe. To him the major focus of life became increasingly the South against the world.

Back at Columbia, the Judge longed to remain indispensable

at the university, where the trustees were more successful at persuading him to stay in office than they had been at Mississippi. He hinted vaguely at retirement a number of times but was always implored to continue the work of his administration. Eventually, he began to argue that he had been importuned to remain in office by the students. He enjoyed the dignity and comforts of his position and was at last growing too old to begin another career.

Harbingers of War

Within six months, however, he was to find his life and goals drastically altered by the encroaching war, for South Carolina seceded from the Union in December 1860. By spring, Georgia, Alabama, Mississippi, and Louisiana followed suit. At first the Judge was delighted since it seemed as if his humiliations at the Methodist and statistical conferences had been vindicated. Then Lamar resigned his congressional seat and expressed grave concern to his father-in-law about the prospect of war. The old man was aghast at the possibility of southern aggression. In panic he wrote to South Carolina's Governor Pickens, deprecating hasty actions, as portions of his letter, dated 30 December 1860, reveal:

For the Lord's sake Governor, if it be possible, prevent a collision with the Federal Government before Alabama and Mississippi get out of the Union. Did any one ever hear of such carryings on as we have at this time! . . . No opening for a rupture would be made until the Federal Government undertook to collect the revenues after we determined not to pay them—or allow them to be collected. In the meantime Alabama, Mississippi, and Florida perhaps Georgia would have been out of the union and formed into a confederacy with us, and Lincoln would have had the whole line of coast to force, with no troops to do it with. The North would be up in arms against him—they would not be taxed to carry on such a war. . . . I would say throw an embankment around Fort Moultrie that will protect it from the heat of Fort Sumter and the cannons of ships of war and hold it quietly, let the duties be collected, and bear patiently any thing but an attack upon the city until we form our Southern Confederacy. Then Buchanan or Lincoln will have too many forts to attend to, to make these alarming. . . . I would say try the Concord and

Lexington experiment as soon as possible; but there is no need of that now; and to attempt it would be in the highest degree imprudent and perilous to our great cause. And yet forgetting the difference of circumstances, this is the very thing that many of our people are driving at. "That will unite the South" say they. Isn't the South (at least all that we care about) uniting just as fast as it possibly can? . . . I write (as my letter shows) in great haste and in great distress, for I greatly fear, that just at the time South Carolina was about to see her highest aspirations realized, I am to see her humiliated. The *ergo* of all I have written is *put off* as long as possible a collision with the Federal *Government*. [At the end of this letter Longstreet added a postscript:]

P.S. Even when you get the Forts, you will be considered as in a state of war and Charleston will be blockaded: what then. I have just heard you propose taking Fort Sumter by a *coup de main*. If it succeeds, *let the first gun be fired by the enemy, not from either fort*.[51]

In the next weeks and months, he would often entreat his fellow southerners not to be the aggressor in any military action. Mercifully, Longstreet never saw the connection between his own separatist views and the sudden threat of war. The college president who had urged his students three years earlier to "let your flight be like that of the eagle . . . [that] strikes with strong wing the angry elements which hurry it away,"[52] now hoped to prevent the conflict his own bombast had helped create. In a pamphlet called "Shall South Carolina Begin the War?" the Judge implored the citizens of his state to avoid the catastrophe of armed battle:

Woe to the people who bring such a conflict but from dire necessity. Is it necessary? No, no, no! It is not only bootless, desperate, but wholly unnecessary. The Black Republicans mean to collect the revenues. This . . . is war in disguise, but practically it is harmless . . . the revenues will be collected at sea. Be it so; let them have them. . . . France and England will enter into treaties of commerce, and open a glorious traffic with us. Thus by a little delay, and the forfeiture of the customs for a few months, we gain everything we desire with the loss of one drop of blood. . . . I implore you let the first shot come from the enemy.[53]

Consciously the Judge hoped his pamphlet would urge judicious behavior on the hotheads. Tacitly, and perhaps unknowingly, he left the door open in the event of "dire necessity." He established the North as a bellicose aggressor, and his warning about not firing the *first* shot, a phrase he had also used in his letter to the governor, implies that he anticipated the worst. At a later time his pamphlet protected his reputation in some circles. Did he not, after all, argue against armed aggression? Surely his loyalty to his region once the war began could never be questioned. While he tried to dissuade the first students at the university from enlisting, the entire student body departed from Columbia without his permission just after the fall of Port Royal. He salvaged the last vestiges of his authority by going to the train station to bless their mission. The Longstreets immediately thereafter packed up their possessions and left for Mississippi. The Judge's career as college administrator had finally come to an end.

Although he had not welcomed the war, Longstreet was anxious to contribute to the southern cause once the fighting had begun. Wade tells how he developed a bizarre plan for disguising himself as a slave, entering a Yankee ship, and blowing it up with dynamite.[54] He even proposed the plan to Lee who tactfully suggested its impracticality. Too old to fight, he was nevertheless physically strong and psychologically primed for action. Most of his activities during the war were frenzied and frequently irrational since he wanted to be helpful, to be a force in the southern effort, but his thinking was often muddled. As a young man, he had divided his activities over a broad field and had quickly tired of each new venture. He was always creative but the clever ideas that came to him so easily seldom seemed engrossing once they had gone beyond the planning stage. At seventy, Longstreet was almost a caricature of the hyperactive, overachieving, eclectic man of affairs.

He wrote continually to his son-in-law, Lamar, and his nephew, James, now equally indispensable leaders in the southern cause. Lamar, who had drafted Mississippi's secession document, served in the Confederate Congress. Then, after a short term as the colonel of a regiment, he was sent as a Confederate envoy to Russia and eventually, in a semiofficial capacity, to England and France. Everywhere his calm, rational demeanor, sharp mind, and perfect manners made him a valuable spokesman for his region. No less important to the southern cause and more actively engaged in combat than Lamar, his cousin-by-marriage James Longstreet served as brigade, division, and corps commander from Bull Run to Antietam. Having served in the United States Army since his graduation from West Point, he resigned at the outbreak of the war and joined the Confederacy. Highly respected as a tactician and admired for his courage, the general commanded Lee's right wing at Gettysburg where he fought valiantly and, in the consensus of most recent historians, effectively.[55]

Longstreet doubtless derived some vicarious satisfaction from his association with his famous kin. In other times when he had been troubled, he depended on his family's closeness to sustain him. Now his daughter, Virginia Lamar, and her children, as well as Mrs. Longstreet, looked to him for moral strength and physical protection. The Longstreets left Mississippi before their house was burned by the Yankees; Mrs. Lamar and her children accompanied her parents to Oxford, Georgia, and the Branhams went to Greensboro, Alabama. Such relocations, difficult for most older people, only stimulated the Judge to further activity. He refused to wait out the war calmly in Oxford but rushed to Charleston, South Carolina, and began a Sunday school for black and white children. Another interracial project he sponsored was a school in Enon, Alabama, near Columbus, Georgia, where he often gave the lessons in mathematics. It seemed that he was trying to be a model of the proslavery aristocrat who paradoxically cared more for the Negroes than did their Yankee emancipators. Perhaps he was consciously or unconsciously justifying his attitudes to his God, to potential critics in the North, or to historians of a later day. In spite of his peripatetic altruism, he found time to counsel as a clergyman and friend the citizens of Columbus, particularly the rich and socially prominent, all members of the class he had once satirized in *Georgia Scenes.*

His nephew must have experienced some dread at the frequency and content of the Judge's letters, always filled with suggestions for military maneuvers and endless directions and plans for conducting the war. For the ordinary soldiers, Longstreet wrote a series of pamphlets called "Valuable Suggestions," designed to discourage fear and build up morale. He published a book in 1864, "on Brown's extra session," or so he wrote in a letter to Lamar. It was subsequently lost.

Acceptance of the End

Early in 1865 the Longstreets returned to Mississippi in anticipation of the war's conclusion. Over a period of years they had received firsthand accounts from their nephew's pen of the tragic loss of life and general weakening of the southern position. Like other southern families, they were stoically prepared for the final defeat, but they were emotionally incapable of comprehending the full tragedy of the experience. Oxford was somewhat less bleak than many other towns since the campus of the university had at least been spared. The Longstreets took a four-room cottage near the Lamars' plantation which had been damaged but was still standing. In 1866 Lamar was given a position at the university where young Waddel was now president. At last Longstreet had the consolation of seeing his chosen successor in command. The Branhams had also returned and there was daily contact among the various branches of the family. General James Longstreet visited occasionally. He was politically more flexible than his uncle, and he shared the old gentleman's love of new projects. Because James was eager to heal the old wounds and begin to build the New South, he was misunderstood in some circles by those who considered reconciliation cowardly or at best callous and opportunistic. Longstreet disagreed with his nephew's views, but he supported him loyally in public.

The older man's own views on society were modeled on Calhoun's philosophy of government, and since the values of the New South were unacceptable to him, he preferred instead to cherish a more Utopian model from the past, one he had discussed personally with Calhoun, who had died in 1850. When Governor Perry of South Carolina, an unpopular Reconstruction politician, wrote an article in 1869 criticizing the late vice-president's political and religious views, Longstreet mounted an angry attack on the governor in a review in the January 1870 issue of the *Nineteenth Century*. There he stated his own and Calhoun's shared vision of a Biblical, patriarchal society:

I believe that he [Calhoun] regarded the government of the children of Israel in the wilderness, the most perfect that ever existed on earth. Be that as it may, he called my attention to it more than once as exactly the government ours ought to be, or was intended to be. "There," said he, "each tribe had its place on the march and in the camp, each managed its own concerns in its own way, neither interfered in the slightest degree, with the private affairs of the other, nor did their common head interfere with any of them in any matters, save such as were of equal interest to all, but unmanageable by them as separate and distinct communities."[56]

Of course, the Judge had found in Calhoun's ideas another justification for states rights. The Judge's mixture of philosophy and politics was later described by Parrington as a "Hebraized concept of a Jeffersonian order."[57]

In social situations, Longstreet was not so defensive and testy. He and Eliza read stories to their grandchildren, visited with neighbors, and played cards. The Judge's depressed spirits following the trauma of the war, and the discomforts and humiliations of Reconstruction, seem to have slowed his life down to a sensible, almost tranquil pace. Even though in theory he had always prized the sanctity of the family above worldly success, his natural talent, vigor, and competitiveness had involved him in an endless series of ambitious enterprises. He cherished family occasions, such as his fiftieth wedding anniversary celebration, and he appears to have remained very close to his wife and to have been dependent on her company till the end. A year after their anniversary Mrs. Longstreet died. He bore the loss well, with a return to a more intense involvement with religion. He began to study Hebrew so that he could conduct Biblical research, and the result of his labors was a book called *A Correction of the Canonized Errors in Biblical Interpretation*. The manuscript was later burned when fire destroyed the home of his literary executor, Edward Mayes, who, while a student in Mississippi, had met and later married Longstreet's granddaughter, Frances Lamar; he was the last of the Judge's promising young protégés, and like one of the first, his father-in-law Lamar, Mayes remained a lifetime admirer of the old gentleman.

To the end, Longstreet retained vestiges of shrewdness and wit. His mind wandered, but his days were structured with projects that required his attention. While the Old South was gone and with it his dream of a vigorous, pious agrarian society, in his children and grandchildren many of his ideals had taken hold and would flourish; in them he had a stake in the future. After a short illness in the summer of 1870, he began to let go of life, confident in his faith that he would soon be joining his wife and the children he had buried many years before. He died on 9 July 1870, surrounded by his daughters and their families.

By any standards Longstreet's personal and professional life was successful. His family adored him for his loving, protective nature, and his friends admired his loyalty, stamina, and versatility. Although taken separately his careers in law, the ministry, and college administration were not unique, in the aggregate they are testaments to a remarkably adventurous spirit. Benevolently domineering, he embodied the virtues of tradition and order for many, especially the students whose lives he sought with the best intentions to mold. At his worst, he was haughty and, in his later years, given to concealing bigoted and self-serving theories in specious philosophical artifice. Too often he surrounded himself with uncritical admirers whose company he preferred to those whose intellectual attainments might be higher than his own. Thus, as it is with most men, his character was a composite of conflicting values and longings. For a humble Christian he was suspiciously fond of worldly renown. He envied national celebrities of his acquaintance, such as Calhoun or even his nephew, James, and his son-in-law, Lamar. He might have been comforted to know that one day he would occupy a modest but permanent niche in American literary history, but he tended to deprecate his own books and stories. His first biographer, Fitzgerald, noted, "It would have jarred upon Judge Longstreet's feeling had he been told while living that he would be most widely known and remembered longest by his 'Georgia Scenes.' "[58]

Chapter Two

Georgia Scenes and the Piedmont South

The printing of *Georgia Scenes* in 1835 by the Sentinel Press provided the first opportunity for readers outside of rural Georgia to read Longstreet's humorous sketches, most of which had previously appeared in Augusta's *State Rights Sentinel* or Milledgeville's *Southern Recorder.* The historical timing of this edition proved to be propitious since the public appetite for stories in a southern setting had been whetted by the Tidewater aristocrats' exciting portraits of plantation life, for example, John Pendleton Kennedy's *Swallow Barn* (1832), a series of sketches in the tradition of Washington Irving's *Bracebridge Hall* (1822). William Gilmore Simms in Georgia and Edgar Allan Poe in Baltimore were using their influence as journalists and editors to promote first-rate literature in their own regions, thereby asserting to the world that southern men of letters were a match for northern writers. In fact, C. Hugh Holman has argued that 1835 was a unique year in the development of southern literature:

The *annus mirabilis* of southern literature was 1835. In that year Augustus Baldwin Longstreet published the book-length collection of sketches of frontier low-life known as *Georgia Scenes;* John Pendleton Kennedy published his popular romance of the Revolution, *Horse-Shoe Robinson,* and further enhanced the glittering reputation he had made with *Swallow Barn;* Edgar Allan Poe published some of his early short stories and assumed the editorship of the *Southern Literary Messenger;* and William Gilmore Simms published in April his romance of Indian warfare in the colonial South, *The Yemassee,* and in December the first of his seven loosely connected romances of the American Revolution, *The Partisan*. Never again was one twelve-month period to represent the Old South so impressively in the literary market place, which had already established itself along an axis represented by the stagecoach route linking Philadelphia and New York City.[1]

Holman recognized that the reading public was prepared to accept a variety of approaches to regional literature. Kennedy's novels continued the Tidewater tradition of romance, Simms's *Yemassee* injected the Indian theme into the southern novel, Poe's exotic, almost Gothic short stories transcended regionalism, and Longstreet's crude, hearty portraits of Georgia crackers, ignored by previous writers, expanded the possibilities of frontier fiction in the Piedmont region.

Prior to 1835, the men with the greatest commitment to the plantation system and to self-government became the literary spokesmen for their region. Much significant antebellum writing therefore had as its focus plantation life. Within the next decades, Philip Pendleton Cooke and his brother, John Esten Cooke, following Kennedy's example, added some glamorous chapters to the plantation legend; the former's stories of Virginia life and the latter's novels, *Leather Stocking and Silk* (1852) and *Virginia Comedians* (1854), exaggerated the virtues of the southern landowner. On the other hand, George W. Bagby in 1859 declared his intention to bring about "the unkind but complete destruction" of John Cooke's reputation, and Virginia's Thomas Nelson Page, commenting after the Civil War, accused Cooke of "writing through the lenses of [Sir Walter] Scott."[2] Bagby later turned romancer himself in "The Old Virginia Gentleman" (1877); in the last quarter of the century, he and Page, years after Longstreet's death, followed the tradition of romance, rather than borrowing from the school of frontier humor initiated by the Judge, and fostered a southern literature of nostalgia for the plantation era.

In the years before the war, William Gilmore Simms was more involved in sponsoring a southern literary tradition than in upholding any one aspect of his region. With James Wright Simmons he founded the *Southern Literary Gazette* to encourage native authors, and his own novels, such as *Martin Faber* (1832), *Beauchampe* (1842), and *Charlemont* (1856), were based on historical incident, as was his most widely read book, *The Yemassee,* already mentioned, which deals with an Indian uprising and is often compared to Cooper's stories of the frontier. Simms believed the future of southern letters depended on a judicious use of local materials to present themes of universal interest. In his preface to *The Wigwam and the Cabin* (1856), he made some prophetic remarks about the proper goals of regional authors:

> To be *national* in literature one must needs be *sectional.* No one mind can fully or fairly illustrate the characteristics of any great country; and he who shall depict one section faithfully, has made his proper and sufficient contribution to the great work of *national* illustration.[3]

Simms nevertheless recognized the need to justify southern institutions to a national reading public. He wrote to Benjamin Franklin Perry that he was supporting the *Southern Quarterly Review* so that "we may have at least one organ among ourselves to which we may turn when it becomes necessary to express Southern feelings and opinions."[4] The *Southern Quarterly Review* supported the social and economic ideals of the plantation system. So, too, did the poetry of Irwin Russell in the 1870s and the short stories of Armistead Gordon early in this century.

Georgia Scenes is in direct contrast with this traditional vision of the South. Longstreet himself was the kind of country gentleman the aristocrats would have admired, but he sought to reveal a part of southern life that they ignored. Tales of the small farmer contributed little to the epic vision of southern life depicted by the romancers. Longstreet thus became one of the first of a small, persistent number of writers who attempted to capture the spirit of the plain people. Most of these writers chose the frontier areas as settings for their stories. The publication of the revised edition of *Georgia Scenes* in 1840 coincided with the appearance of William Tappan Thompson's *Major Jones's Courtship,* a comic story composed of letters describing episodes in rural Georgia. Later Richard Malcolm Johnston and Charles Henry Smith ("Bill Arp") created additional legends of middle Georgia, and Joel Chandler Harris was to become a major contributor to the local color movement during the last quarter of the nineteenth century.

Robert Phillips has written that Longstreet and these other Georgia writers vacillated between romance and realism, adding that "they were not willing to examine and expose the area and its people with consistent honesty."[5] They were willing, however, to depict the harsh lives of people who lived on the outer edges of civilization.

Longstreet's Masterpiece

Although the stories of *Georgia Scenes* were written and printed separately, there is justification for evaluating the book as one complete work. Wade and Fitzgerald argue that the author carelessly assembled his finest book, and it has been noted that he had monumental distractions in his personal and professional life. Yet the sense of a unique vision of southern life, the generally affirmative analysis of a cultural phenomenon, depends on the cumulative effect of the tales.

Individually, few, if any, of Longstreet's sketches would be known today had they not been collected in one volume. The stories in the *Southern Recorder* or *States Rights Sentinel* reached a tiny audience, whereas *Georgia Scenes* became a literary landmark.

For example, when Longstreet first began to publish his sketches, he signed them either "Hall" or "Baldwin" with no apparent reason for choosing these names; they were merely pen names that provided anonymity. When these sketches were collected in *Georgia Scenes*, however, "Hall" and "Baldwin" ceased to be arbitrary pseudonyms; instead, each took on a distinct persona, representing divergent aspects of Georgia life. Although the stories will be discussed separately, their links to one another and to the major themes of the book will also be explored.

Nineteen Stories Make a Book

"Georgia Theatrics," written sometime in 1833, became the lead story in the collection. It is a pleasant tale which, like many of the sketches in *Georgia Scenes,* depends upon a single basic trick for its plot and theme. On a June morning in 1809, the narrator, Hall, overhears what he guesses is a fierce struggle between two men in the thicket beside a country road in Lincolnton County:

> In Mercy's name! thought I, what band of ruffians has selected this holy season and this heavenly retreat for such Pandaemonian riots! I quickened my gait, and had come nearly opposite to the thick grove whence the noise proceeded, when my eye caught indistinctly, and at intervals, through the foliage of the dwarf-oaks and hickories which intervened, glimpses of a man or men, who seemed to be in a violent struggle; and I could occasionally catch those deep-drawn, emphatic oaths which men in conflict utter when they deal blows. (10)

Hall's pretended shock at overhearing foul language and his hyperbolic comparison of the fracas with Milton's Pandemonium establishes him as the educated, amused, teasing storyteller. Dismounting with the intention of breaking up the fight, he can see through the foliage only one of the contestants loudly bragging that he has gouged out his opponent's eye. Horror-struck, Hall chastises the young man for his savagery, charging him to aid his "fellow mortal," whom he has "ruined forever." Much to the relief of the reader and the embarrassment of Hall and the youth, the maimed victim is a figment of the boy's imagination. Hall had stumbled on a rehearsal of some pretended fight in which the fantasizing adolescent plays both roles himself. The satire on masculine vanity and competitiveness is softened by Hall's consideration of the boy's youthful spirit. The narrator reveals that he doesn't mind a joke on himself and that he has an amused tolerance of adolescent diversion. One recalls young Gus's love of jumping, boxing, and running, and he was probably called upon more than once to defend himself against class bullies at Waddel's academy.

Wade suggests that the story may be an allusion to "Don Quixote charging at the windmills" and comments that after the Civil War "Georgia Theatrics" was read before Congress in order to demonstrate the folly of hasty, misguided judgments during sectional debates. Later the sketch was included in *Colonel Crockett's Exploits and Adventures in Texas* (1860), where it was taken as a pointed commentary on Andrew Jackson's attack upon the United States Bank. Whatever the deeper significance of the story, "Georgia Theatrics" is a pleasing introduction to

Longstreet's fictional world with an authentic quality which stimulates the reader's interest in the judge's travels and experiences; it also serves as a warning to readers not to take him too seriously, to see him as a trickster as well as a social historian. Furthermore, it hints that the author was aware of conflicts in his own quarrelsome, competitive nature.

Appearing in the *Southern Recorder* on 29 October 1833, "The Dance" is the first scene, according to Wade, that Longstreet published. It is a detailed introduction to the life of a middle Georgian and a more self-conscious rendering of the ways of simple rural people than "Theatrics." In the former sketch, Longstreet had been amused by the exuberance of youth, and in his nature and actions the feisty country boy was not especially distinguished from his urban cousins. "The Dance," on the other hand, provides a deliberate contrast between the rudimentary but wholesome pleasures of country folk and the joyless affectations of the narrator's social peers in the city.

Baldwin is the narrator this time, and his nostalgia for the dances of his own youth—such as "the good old republican six reel"—is linked with his disdain for the morals and manners of the city. At the same time, his emphasis on the social distance between himself and the country people he is describing make him a very stiff, moralizing traditionalist.

Holman has noted that a conscious intellectual and social gulf between author-narrators and the frontier characters they describe is a characteristic of Piedmont fiction and that chroniclers of the region share "a remarkable unanimity of opinion and attitude towards its inhabitants,"[6] finding them laughable, distorted outcasts of civilization. On *Georgia Scenes,* Holman comments:

Here the detached view of a cultivated lawyer and judge established a vantage point which gave aesthetic distance to his portraits of the cruel, learned, but shrewd denizens of the piedmont, weighing these people against the implicit concept of the ordered seaboard society which Judge Longstreet revered. As a result the figures in *Georgia Scenes* are comic grotesques.[7]

In fact, the narrators of *Georgia Scenes,* Hall and Baldwin, both maintain the aesthetic distance Holman describes, but they are products of slightly contrasting backgrounds and hence their characters are portrayed from diverging perspectives. Hall is the country aristocrat, recognized as a "gentleman" by simple folk but respected for his hardy masculinity. Baldwin's tendency to analyze the intricacies of society suggests that despite his satirical jibes at modern foppery he is more comfortable in urban drawing rooms than in the pine barrens. The humor of "The Dance" depends upon the incongruity of finding Baldwin at a country dance although he approves the old-fashioned reels; and the basic joke of the story is that the distinguished judge remembers that he once was infatuated with Polly Gibson, his host's wife, whereas the lady is unable to remember him at all.

Unlike most of this narrator's stories, "The Dance" takes place in the country, but the simplicity and wholesomeness of rural life frequently serves to remind him of urban affectations of dress or manner. For example, he praises country girls at the expense of their city cousins:

The refinements of the present day in female dress had not even reached our republican *cities* at this time; and, of course, the *country girls* were wholly ignorant of them. They carried no more cloth upon their arms or straw upon their heads than was necessary to cover them. They used no artificial means of spreading their frock tails to an interesting extent from their ankles. They had no boards laced to their breasts, nor any corsets laced to their sides; consequently, they look, for all the world, like human beings, and could be distinctly recognized as such at a distance of two hundred paces. Their movements were as free and active as nature would permit them to be. Let me not be understood as interposing the least objection to any lady in this land of liberty dressing just as she pleases. If she choose to lay her neck and shoulders bare, what right have I to look at them? much less to find fault with them. If she choose to put three yards of muslin in a frock sleeve, what right have I to ask why a little strip of it was not put in the body? If she like the pattern of a hoisted umbrella for a frock, and the shape of a cheese-cask for her body, what is all that to me? (14)

Clearly, Baldwin suggests that the bare shoulders of city women are immodest and that their excessive use of fabric on other parts of their clothing is ludicrously extravagant.

As a satirist, Longstreet is often so heavy-handed that his criticism lacks style or bite. Furthermore, none of his narrators can use irony or derisive humor without explicating their didactic purposes, and one assumes that Longstreet shared this failing. Baldwin is fond of mimicking the artificiality of affluent young men and women of his own time, particularly of the women. When he describes a typical city girl he always refers to her sarcastically as a "charming creature" and gives her a silly, pretentious name like "Octavia Matilda Juliana Claudia Ipecacuanha." Baldwin's reflection on Miss Ipecacuanha's amusement at the hour when the waiting dancers assemble—"dressed for a ball at nine in the morning!"—is inevitably followed by a head-shaking retort: "And what have you to say against it? If people must dance, is it not much more rational to employ the hour allotted to exercise in that amusement than the hours sacred to repose and meditation?" (p. 13)

The narrator's indignation spoils the lighthearted tone that initiates his description of the dance. It would have been possible to argue that country people were unaffected without overemphasizing their piety. The girls are "attired in manufactures of their own hands." They disdain the extravagant use of material that characterizes dress in the cities and corseting that might obscure their "natural" appearance. The guests at the country dance shake hands when they meet, unlike city folk, who greet their friends with a kiss, a habit that was lamentably borrowed from the French, Baldwin notes, adding "and by them from Judas." The word *Fashionables* is, in fact, italicized to underscore the narrator's contempt for the beau monde. While Baldwin sometimes captures fragments of native Georgia speech that possess authenticity and freshness, the dialogue he records often seems unbelievably quaint. Perhaps Georgians really did use expressions like "Ding my buttons," but occasionally such rural idioms seem incongruous.

Baldwin discovers pastoral beauty and purity in the country dance which transports him into a world of nostalgic recollections as forgotten memories cause him to question both the ambitions that once propelled him to scorn a simple life and the warped priorities of his present existence.

I was foolishly told that my talents were of too high an order to be employed in the drudgeries of a farm, and I more foolishly believed it. I forsook the pleasures which I had tried and proved, and went in pursuit of those imaginary joys which seemed to encircle the seat of Fame. From that moment to the present, my life had been little else than one unbroken scene of disaster, disappointment, vexation, and toil. And now, when I was too old to enjoy the pleasures which I had discarded, I found that my aim was absolutely hopeless; and that my pursuits had only served to unfit me for the humbler walks of life, and to exclude me from the higher. (18)

There are few other moments in *Georgia Scenes* when Baldwin expresses his personal frustrations so openly. Generally, he is composed, judgmental, quick to point out the waste and disorder of other people's lives; his personal despondency here is unexpected but touching. Longstreet may be using Baldwin to show that even the most self-assured, respected people experience feelings of inadequacy and confusion. He may be speaking through his narrator to confess his own boredom and disappointment, or to suggest that the achievements of his public life, admired by so many Georgians, have failed to satisfy him. The author-narrator mask seldom slips, but when it does, the highly likable face behind it is tantalizing. Baldwin, whom the author casts as a bachelor, did not have the support of a woman like Frances Eliza Longstreet or of two devoted daughters. Although he was aware of worldly disappointments, Longstreet was always properly appreciative of the emotional support his family provided.

Baldwin not only shares some of Longstreet's attitudes; he also, like the author, considers himself physically unattractive. Although Wade described Longstreet's appearance as impressive, he was by no stretch of the imagination a handsome man. The few daguerrotypes that have been salvaged indicate he bore a resemblance to Abraham Lincoln, with his exceedingly long, gaunt face. Neither of the Judge's early biographers reports that his appearance made a negative impression, though Jennette Tandy, writing long after his death, called him "notoriously ugly."[8] Longstreet's self-evaluation is the relevant issue here, not whether others found him attractive or homely nor whether they good-naturedly teased him about his plainness. Through Baldwin and other characters in his fiction, Longstreet acknowledges the hurt that negative comments about his homely appearance had caused him. Usually such remarks are made in jest, but the reader is left to imagine the character's defensive reaction. Squire Gibson's comment that his wife "never could have loved such a hard-favored man as you are" is the first of the many references to Baldwin's homeliness. Baldwin and Ned Brace, who appears later in the stories as a bizarre comic figure, and John Brown in *William Mitten* are all hard-favored men who tend to compensate for their lack of good looks by incessantly ridiculing their appearance or by initiating cruel jokes on themselves, as if to anticipate rejection and disfavor, consequently turning what they dread to some possible advantage. Similarly, Longstreet's jokes at Yale about Georgia crackers had helped turn his rural background into a social asset. He had discovered that the person who humiliates himself inspires an indulgent attitude in his audience, whose laughter is possibly interpreted as a sign of approval.

"The Dance" is a successful story because it assimilates both the narrator's need to be the object of a joke and his need to prove the moral superiority of simple Georgia country folk. The fact that Baldwin remembers Mrs. Gibson as the sweetheart of his youth, while she fails to recognize him, may suggest that the narrator has exaggerated the intensity of his youthful passions with the passage of time. The successful judge who is at ease in the city's finest drawing rooms and is sought after by the social lion hunters finds himself anonymous at an unpretentious country dance and unable to establish a link with the past he cherishes in memory. After cataloging the practicality, wholesome charm, and charitable nature of Mrs. Gibson and the other country women, Baldwin provides his most convincing example of their special attractiveness. Mrs. Gibson, deficient in the urban arts of coquetry, refuses to pretend, merely in order to be polite, that she remembers a man when she does not. With warmth and rough but compassionate honesty, she clearly states that she cannot remember the judge, and even her husband's note to Baldwin later is still firm on this point: "Since you left her, Polly has been thinking about the old times, and, she says, to save her life, she can't recollect you." (22) Baldwin wisely concludes his narrative with the squire's letter, combining successfully the lighthearted humor and moral lesson of his tale.

In "The Horse-Swap," Hall is once more narrator and the tale has the flavor of frontier humor. The story first appeared in the *Southern Recorder* on 13 November 1833. A sense of the burning Georgia sun on cracked red clay and the coarse jesting of hard-working country folk pervades this almost archetypal anecdote of horse trading. The swap is a form of recreation for some Georgians, a way of life for others. The horse swap is a male event and it tends to attract farmer and city slicker alike, fools, braggarts, and con artists. In a swap there is always suspense, overt or masked power play, rhetoric, humor, and ultimate victory for one of its participants. The rules of the swap are established by tradition and instinct, and at times they seem as ritualistic and complex as the Japanese dance; surely the most admired stance of the combatants is a kind of relaxed inscrutability. As with the merchant and customer who bargain over any piece of merchandise, the horse trader must measure his risks and gauge when to be aggressive, when to compromise or retreat. It takes a gambler's instinct and a poker face to win at horse swapping, and even the wiliest participant knows that luck may desert him. Hall's description of the horse swap is a good example of a basically familiar situation described with skill and imagination. Mark Twain's "Celebrated Jumping Frog of Calavaras County" (1865) comes to mind as a comparable tale. Both stories begin with the ritualistic boasting of the adversaries, a pattern in the Anglo-Saxon literary tradition we can trace back to Beowulf and Unferth, and both employ narrators whose personal discomfort in frontier surroundings is a source of additional comedy. Mark Twain's unnamed narrator is himself the victim of a hoax. Sent on a mission to find Leonidas W. Smiley, he realizes that such a gentleman probably never existed. A playful friend had counted on "garrulous," old Simon Wheeler's recalling a Jim Smiley and subjecting the unwitting stranger to a full account of the latter's adventures. Thus, there are two victims of practical jokes in the story, the narrator and the gambler in Wheeler's anecdote who bets on a jumping frog only to discover its jowls have been packed with buckshot. Of course, "The Celebrated Jumping Frog of Calavaras County" provides a more sustained and obvious treatment of the narrator as a figure of fun, but the anomaly of finding Longstreet's narrator, a highly educated, "evolved" Georgian in primitive surroundings adds to the charm of "The Horse-Swap" and *Georgia Scenes* in general.

In "The Horse-Swap," Hall looks on while a character named
Yellow Blossom initiates the swapping ritual with his claim that
he is "perhaps a leetle, just a *leetle,* of the best man at a horse-
swap that ever trod shoe leather." Peter Ketch and his son
Neddy accept the challenge. Ketch is a modest, quiet man who
masks the shrewdness and cunning that guarantee his eventual
success. Yet even though it is possible to anticipate the comeup-
pance of the braggart Yellow Blossom, suspense surrounds every
cautious move he and his adversaries make. Yellow Blossom's
skinny, skeletal Bullet is pitted against Ketch's Kit, a smoother
looking sorrel. Ketch immediately boasts of Kit's blindness, an
admission that seems naive at first unless we sense that such
unexpected openness may be a means of putting Yellow Blossom
off guard. As tradition demands, the crucial first bid asserts
the superiority of the trader's present horse and requires a cash
supplement for any trading agreement. Each man increases his
boasts about the prowess of his own horse and the inadequacy
of his opponent's. Yet the ethics of horse swapping demand
that a man not lie about his horse's shortcomings but merely
omit crucial data that could damage his market value. Also he
must hold in reserve some derisive remarks about the animal
after he finally trades it; therefore, positive and negative attributes of each animal are phrased with care, since each man
must reverse his position in regard to each horse after the trade
has been realized.

Eventually when Yellow Blossom hands Peter Ketch three
dollars and the horse trade is at last accomplished, the cunning
seller reveals a huge sore in Bullet's back which, Hall comments,
"seemed to have defied all medical skill." As we expect, Ketch
is humiliated by the scorn and crude jesting of the onlookers.
Rising to his father's defense, after watching Yellow Blossom
savor the crowd's insults to his adversary and the praises to
his own cleverness, young Ned Ketch delivers the ultimate put-
down: "His [Bullet's] back's mighty bad off; but dad drot my
soul if he's put it to daddy as bad as he thinks he has, for old
Kit's both blind and *deef,* I'll be drot if he ein't." The laconic
father at last has the opportunity for a wry witticism, all the
more effective because of the taunts that provoked it: "If you
can only get Kit rid of them little failings you'll find him all
sorts of a horse" (30–31).

As a tale that reveals the competitive nature of men, their special vanities and basic vulnerability, "The Horse-Swap" deserves to be rated as one of Longstreet's finest. Here he describes the inhabitants of his region without the moralizing patronage that mars so many of his tales. His best anecdotal gifts are blended here with his psychological intuition to produce classic frontier humor. Vernon Louis Parrington enjoyed "The Horse-Swap," and Edgar Allan Poe, reviewing *Georgia Scenes* in 1836 for the *Southern Literary Messenger,* was effusive in his praise of the story, which he called "most excellent in every respect— but especially so in its delineations of Southern bravado, and the keen sense of the ludicrous evinced in the portraiture of the steeds." Poe added that he considered the description of Bullet "superior, in joint humor and verisimilitude, to anything of the kind we have ever seen."[9]

Poe's evaluation of the next story in *Georgia Scenes* was less favorable. He was amused by "Character of a Native Georgian," which had first been published in January of 1834, but did not believe that it was "so good as the scenes which precede or succeed it." The central character of the piece, Ned Brace, seemed to be "neither very original, nor appertaining exclusively to Georgia."[10] Another critic writing in Longstreet's lifetime, James Wood Davidson, defended the characterization to the point of insisting that "Ned Brace and his adventures, oddities and drolleries make up the most amusing portion of the book."[11] Ned is introduced to the reader by Hall, who describes his friend as an eccentric country squire, overly fond of practical jokes and often projecting an image of madness. Just as little Gus Longstreet's childhood willfulness and disruptive spirit had caused his beleaguered teacher to believe the boy was insane, so, too, Ned's erratic behavior alarms strangers unaccustomed to his fool's pose. But Ned is more than a comedian and show-off. He represents that part of Longstreet's nature, aggressive and exhibitionistic, that the Judge would never quite repress. Hall, as an earthy country aristocrat, and Baldwin, as a conservative, somewhat priggish judge, personify qualities of the author that he found socially acceptable. Ned's character hints at a third, unruly side to the Judge's nature. In the modern parlance he is Longstreet's "id," whereas Hall and Baldwin are "super-ego" figures. Like Ned, Longstreet was a consummate put-on artist, a sometimes brutal tease, an unruly aggressive clown pursued by subtle and ultimately unfathomable demons.

Hall's tolerance of Ned Brace in his character sketch will not necessarily be shared by the reader, who may find him gross, sadistic, infantile. Hall comments that he had known Ned "from his earliest manhood to his grave." Perhaps Ned's rash qualities are ones Longstreet associated with his youth and that had been conquered and hence no longer had "life." At least they provide insights into Longstreet's special brand of humor and provide clues to his attitudes toward people—both in literature and in life.

Ned, according to Hall, "lived only to amuse himself with his fellow-beings" and was able to derive "some gratification of his favorite propensity" from every person he encountered. This avowal of Ned's intention to make individuals serve his constant need for amusement contributes to a compelling portrait of a very eccentric, insecure young man. Ned is declared to be a satirist and hence a moralist, temperamentally akin to Hall and Baldwin. He specializes in teasing the fop, the pedant, the purse-proud, the overfastidious and sensitive. Thus, Longstreet attempted in part to justify aspects of Ned's and possibly his own behavior, which other people considered rude and irritating.

In Hall's narrative, Ned requests that Hall pretend to be a stranger to him while they visit at a country inn. Therefore, the other guests freely discuss Ned with Hall, and the latter gains an objective view of their responses to his friend's personality. Ned's attempts to attract attention to himself may seem more pathetic than amusing. When asked his name, he writes it on a piece of paper (so as to appear a mute), thereby making his first bid for recognition. Then he walks in and out of the bar, observing the disquieting effect of his purposeless entrances and exits on the other guests. But Ned saves his major claim to notoriety until dinner when he requests tea and coffee to drink simultaneously and stirs and pounds all his food to the "consistency of a hard poultice." In addition to his poor table manners, Ned also displays an awesome gluttony so that the entire dining room is either aghast at or uproariously amused by him, depending on how seriously they regard etiquette. To appease the innkeeper's angry wife, whose good services he has imposed on throughout the meal with unreasonable requests, Ned intimately confesses the presence of a past secret which, if revealed, could account for his gross behavior. Touched by his "confession," the gullible woman forgives him immediately and offers to serve future meals in his room.

The unexpected appearance of a stranger provides Ned with the next opportunity for aggressive behavior. Described somewhat contemptuously by Hall as a flighty and smirky little Frenchman, the wayfarer finds himself the center of a commotion when Ned pretends to recognize him. With an affectionate outburst, Ned professes that the Frenchman is an old friend, Mr. Squeezelfanter. (Ridiculous names are an essential characteristic of Longstreet's particular brand of humor.) The Frenchman's protest that he is in fact Jacques Sancric leads Ned to assert that he knew the gentleman was from Sandy Creek and to explore the absurdities of such an association. The discomfort of the stranger and Ned's seemingly preposterous mistaking of a man who can barely speak English for a native Georgian result in a ludicrous scene. In a later episode, Ned's feigned hearing difficulties again result in a comic mistake, which Hall gleefully details:

About four o'clock in the afternoon, while he was standing at the tavern door, a funeral procession passed by, at the foot of which, and singly, walked one of the smallest men I ever saw. As soon as he came opposite the door, Ned stepped out and joined him with great solemnity. The contrast between the two was ludicrously striking, and the little man's looks and uneasiness plainly showed that he felt it. However, he soon became reconciled to it. They proceeded but a little way before Ned inquired of his companion who was dead.

"Mr. Noah Bills," said the little man.

"Nan?" said Ned, raising his hand to his ear in token of deafness, and bending his head to the speaker.

"Mr. Noah Bills," repeated the little man, loud enough to disturb the two couples immediately before him.

"Mrs. Noel's Bill!" said Ned, with mortification and astonishment. "Do the white persons pay such respect to Niggers in Savannah?" (46–47)

According to Hall, the entire funeral procession was convulsed with laughter over Ned's remark. Ned's racism is, of course, one of his most unattractive traits to the modern reader. His baiting an old black woman selling chickens is equally tasteless and even more revealing of the brutality that lies close to the surface of every practical joker's humor. Ned's deliberate singing off-key in church in order to shatter the solemnity of that occasion and his immoderate drinking from a bucket of water needed to smother a fire are hardly more ingratiating examples of his comic sense.

Yet as offensive as he is at times, Ned at last seems to possess a degree of self-knowledge and his eventual confession to the innkeeper's wife reveals a muted cry of pain: "Humor has been my besetting sin. It has sunk me far below the station to which my native gifts entitled me. It has robbed me of all my acquaintances, and, what is much more to be regretted, the esteem of some of my best and most indulgent friends" (49). And although Ned is obviously seeking the lady's sympathy and tolerance, he seems sincere when he refers to his "self-destroying propensity," which he admits is ungovernable. Ned is a caricature of the "funny man" we can find in any society. Longstreet himself, while sharing a similar love of practical jokes, certainly never possessed any trait that could be labeled "ungovernable," yet he reveals his empathetic understanding of the incomplete individual who must make use of other men to prove his own worth.

In "The Fight," Hall continues as narrator, describing with relish a savage battle between two rural strong men. The tone of the story, which first appeared in the *Southern Recorder* on 27 November 1833, recalls the mood of England's post-Restoration drama where the amorality and bawdiness of the plays associated with Charles II's theater was continued but placed in a moralizing or sentimental context. Audiences could vicariously enjoy the protagonist's wickedness during the first two acts and yet experience the even greater luxury of seeing the libertine punished or repentant before the final curtain. There is a primitive vitality to the actual fight in which Bob Durham loses his left ear and in retaliation bites off Bill Stallion's nose, and Hall reveals a wilder comic sense than the reader has heretofore encountered in the *Scenes.*

It would be easy to condemn Hall for the misogyny and snobbery which become readily apparent in his scornful portrayal of idle, malicious wives who urge their husbands to fight and in his amusing but contemptuous description of "white trash" Ransy Sniffle:

Now there happened to reside in the county just alluded to a little fellow by the name of Ransy Sniffle: a sprout of Richmond, who, in his earlier days, had fed copiously upon red clay and blackberries. This diet had given to Ransy a complexion that a corpse would have disdained to own, and an abdominal rotundity that was quite unprepossessing. Long spells of the fever and ague, too, in Ransy's youth, had conspired with clay and blackberries to throw him quite out of the order of nature. His shoulders were fleshless and elevated; his head large and flat; his neck slim and translucent; and his arms, hands, fingers, and feet were lengthened out of all proportion to the rest of his frame. His joints were large and his limbs small; and as for flesh, he could not, with propriety, be said to have any. Those parts which nature usually supplies with the most of this article—the calves of the legs, for example—presented in him the appearance of so many well-drawn blisters. His height was just five feet nothing; and his average weight in blackberry season, ninety-five. I have been thus particular in describing him, for the purpose of showing what a great matter a little fire sometimes kindleth. There was nothing on this earth which delighted Ransy so much as a fight. He never seemed fairly alive except when he was witnessing, fomenting, or talking about a fight. Then, indeed, his deep-sunken gray eye assumed something of a living fire, and his tongue acquired a volubility that bordered upon eloquence. Ransy had been kept for more than a year in the most torturing suspense as to the comparative manhood of Billy Stallings and Bob Durham. He had resorted to all his usual expedients to bring them in collision, and had entirely failed. (54–55)

Sniffle's repulsiveness and the brutality of the fight itself are sources of the story's power, and the conspiracy among Sniffle and Stallion's and Durham's wives that initiates the fight is only a plot contrivance. The reader's enjoyment of the ensuing violence is enhanced by Hall's pretense at shock and dismay, because the narrator, perhaps like the reader, seems ludicrously out of place in a backcountry brawl.

Attempting to place a moral on his bloodthirsty tale, Hall concludes that "thanks to the Christian religion . . . to schools, colleges and benevolent associations, such scenes of barbarism and cruelty . . . are now of rare occurrence." He adds that such fights are a "disgrace to that community" (64). Somehow the tone of Hall's protest is inconsistent with his exuberant glee in describing every brutal detail of the fight and seems possibly ironic. Is he mocking the incorrigibility of the rural poor and the squeamishness of readers with no experience of "common" people?

"The Fight" has evoked a variety of conflicting responses over the years. Poe emphasized the verisimilitude of the sketch, calling it "unsurpassed . . . in the vivid truth to nature of one or two of the personages introduced [especially Ransy Sniffle] . . . and in its generic delineations of real existences to be found sparsely in Georgia, Mississippi and Louisiana, and very plentifully in our more remote settlements and territories."[12] Tandy considered the two combatants' final apologies to each other a "fine drollery."[13] Of all the *Scenes,* Parrington favored this one which he called the "most indigenous to the Georgia frontier, the truest local document."[14] But writing from a more modern perspective, Sylvia Jenkins Cook has deplored the social stereotyping of Georgia crackers by Longstreet's stories and George Washington Harris's Sut Lovingood tales in which the poor man "was a confirmed object of ridicule," adding that these authors had only "an incidental concern with the financial and social burdens of the poor white but a major interest in his grotesque appearance and vicious conduct."[15]

It is possible to argue that with Sniffle Longstreet became one of the first writers to portray the southern grotesque, or misfit, which Faulkner to some extent and Flannery O'Connor to an even greater degree were to use so effectively in twentieth-century fiction. Unsavory characters and brutal situations appear less frequently in nineteenth-century southern plantation fiction. Yet the fiction of the Deep South and of the Piedmont during the same era is full of people and events meant to shock a genteel reading audience, and the presence of grotesques in *Georgia Scenes* and other later works dealing with southern life bring a sense of realism to the fiction. This realism was nearly always diminished by a moralizing authorial intrusion, however, so that a naive reader would not assume that the lusty retelling of crude incidents implied the narrator's approval. It may be an oversimplification to say that Baldwin is more likely to express nostalgia for the simpler, rougher life of early frontier days whereas Hall is more likely to take pride in the gradual civilizing of Georgia, but in the case of "The Fight," at least, the humor of the piece is blended with Hall's awareness of what he calls "the moral darkness" of the frontier. By using two narrators, Longstreet was able to express some of the ambiguity he himself felt toward middle Georgia. He appreciated the "natural" man who in his struggle to survive eschewed the refinements of a more complex society, yet he seemed to feel that the political and social leaders of the state should have experienced the advantage of education and pleasures of civilized society.

"The Fight" indicates that Longstreet acknowledged both the humor and the horror of frontier experience as he depicts a primitive, male ritual against a believable background so that not even Hall's occasionally elegant diction or disapproval diminishes the energy of the scene.

Following this extravagant tale of Georgia low life, Baldwin's recounting the affectations of urban fashionables in regard to prevailing musical tastes again reminds us that a golden mean of behavior, neither too coarse nor too refined, came closest to Longstreet's ideal. Baldwin begins "The Song," written for the *Southern Recorder*'s 8 November 1833 issue, with a diatribe against the vogue of French and Italian music in America. Only the Scottish musicians are truly pleasing to him although the Irish have contributed passably to the fine arts. He expresses particular horror that boarding-school misses can be heard singing French and Italian melodies in "the very language of these nations." A knowledge of classics and of certain major English writers may be essential to a Georgia gentleman and a familiarity with music desirable when restricted to simple country airs, but Baldwin perceives danger in an education that is too far-reaching. Longstreet himself, we recall, was wary of continental influences and despite his wife's pleadings refused to take her to Europe. Women, he seemed to feel, were particularly susceptible to corrupting cultural trends, and like many nineteenth-century Americans, he equated the style and elegance of the Latin countries with effeminacy. Women who eschew the fashionable are always singled out for commendations in Longstreet's work. So it is fitting that Baldwin would praise the singing of Mrs. Mary Williams at a social gathering he attended with his roommate, Hall. The girl's unpretentious name is an indication of the narrator's immediate approval. Names like "Mary" and "John Brown" connote simplicity and purity to Longstreet, and Mary's charm and virtue are further established by her selection of lively Scotch and Irish airs.

In contrast to plain Mary, Baldwin juxtaposes Aurelia Emma Thedosia Augusta Crump, "who had been taught to sing by Madame Piggisqueaki, who was a pupil of Ma'm'celle Crokefroggetta," and had studied piano with Seignor Buzzifussi. Baldwin's satire is childishly crude, though it is not far removed from the philistinism of Mark Twain in *Innocents Abroad*—but without Twain's intentional irony. Miss Crump is portrayed as a bore who does not know when to stop playing her large repertoire of French and Italian songs, and Baldwin's disgust with her reflects his impatience with the affectations of the newly prosperous Georgians, who find it necessary to go to Philadelphia for an education or who turn to Rome and Paris instead of the British Isles for cultural leadership. In this episode Baldwin also criticizes immodesty in dress (Miss Crump's neckline is too low) though his description of the young men's rapt attention to her décolletage and his own suffering during the amateur recitals are among the more amusing passages in the tale. What may be most important about "The Song" for present critics of *Georgia Scenes* is that it reveals the two narrators are very much a part of an increasingly sophisticated Georgia society which they are beginning to distrust.

After providing this glimpse of contemporary decadence, *Georgia Scenes* reverts to the more colorful wholesome past, a more "manly" era when such cultural excesses were inappropriate. "The Turn Out," as narrated by Hall, returns to a man's world and goes back in time at least forty years from the previous story. Appearing in the *Southern Recorder* on 11 December 1833, it is one of the most successful stories in the collection. It relates both an amusing account of a schoolmaster's attempt to regain his captured one-room schoolhouse and an understanding view of interaction between the young and the old on the frontier.

A better known treatment of the same topic, Edward Eggleston's novel, *The Hoosier Schoolmaster* (1870), may possibly owe a debt to "The Turn Out" since Eggleston's book followed *Georgia Scenes* by more than three decades. Eggleston was preoccupied with frontier life, as Longstreet was, and, like the Georgian, he was also a Methodist minister. His book is a part of the post–Civil War local color movement and is more firmly realistic than *Georgia Scenes,* but Longstreet conveys rather deftly in his short piece an amused but sympathetic glimpse of frontier education. Hall's description of the egg-dyeing during Easter week and the egg-picking games that followed provides a pleasing vignette of rural life. Having no toys, the boys use eggs as they might have used marbles, to roll and strike their opponent's eggs: "Egg was struck against egg, point to point, and the egg that was broken was given up as lost to the owner of the one which came back whole from the shock" (74).

The boys express themselves as artists when they decorate their eggs; and afterward their natural competitiveness is sublimated in a harmless game where the winner earns the practical reward of cracked but usable eggs. Hall notes that one of the boys first substituted a wooden egg but was forced to return his ill-gained booty. Later the same boy won the most eggs fairly. Hall refrains here from moralizing, and we are left to draw our own conclusions about the lesson—the boys were taught by the experience.

The central event of "The Turn Out" is the barring of the schoolmaster from the schoolhouse, according to Hall a traditional event in the frontier community when boys, parents, and teachers feel the need for a brief vacation. Rather than declare a scheduled number of holidays, the townspeople choose to ritualize the experience of earning a vacation by testing the strength of schoolmaster and students. Some parents are at hand to referee and ensure justice and prevent violence. It is assumed in advance that the schoolmaster will be forced to permit the holiday, for we are told he is "glad to be turned out," but he must demonstrate his cunning and strength in handling the boys. They in turn must display their own ingenuity and courage in repulsing his attacks on the locked schoolhouse door. Interestingly, the master proves his strength and authority and the children the right to challenge this authority, if only in a game with rules and chaperones. The impression gained from Hall's narrative is of a harmonious community, content with simple pastimes, understanding the needs of each generation, mutually bound in hard work with a sense of fairness and humor. Nostalgia enters in a previously noted passage when Hall comments that years later this rich landscape, apparently abandoned by its inhabitants, became "barren, dreary, and cheerless" (76). The sense of loss is affecting here, and Hall appears momentarily to be grappling with the enigma of change. Throughout "The Turn Out" the writing is subtler and more questioning than in most of *Georgia Scenes*—as if Longstreet were asking us, "Why have we lost so much that was good?"

A sense of lost values certainly pervades "The Charming Creature as Wife," printed first on 14 April 1834 in the *States Rights Sentinel*. Baldwin again attacks the emerging middle class in a sketch twice as long as "The Turn Out." The background and courtship of George Baldwin, the narrator's nephew, and Evelina Smith is extremely detailed, more like the opening of a novel. Then, as if Baldwin has grown weary of his subject matter, and certainly after most readers will have lost patience with it, he contrives an abrupt termination of the tale, mentioning almost in passing that Evelina's poor management of her home suddenly drove her husband to alcoholism and a drunkard's death. Twenty years later, *William Mitten* was to end in a similarly unsatisfying, peremptory manner.

Like so many of Longstreet's stories, "The Charming Creature" is primarily a moral treatise, this time on the need for proper household management, with subthemes involving spoiled children and the affectations of the nouveau riche. In a sense it is a companion piece to *William Mitten*, because both plots involve nephews who refuse to heed their uncles' advice and pay the price in an early death. One wonders why this weakling nephew motif intrigued Longstreet since his own nephew, James, was successful and later a famous Civil War hero. Of course, both "Charming Creature" and *William Mitten* were written when James Longstreet was still a boy, charming, good-looking, but a poor student. The austerity of the West Point education which Longstreet arranged for his nephew was perhaps the necessary chastening experience in the young soldier's life. The unsympathetic uncles in both works see the corrupting influence of wealth and social climbing as background causes of their nephews' tragedies.

Longstreet's distrust of physically attractive people also influences the two works. Evelina is described as a mesmerizing beauty whom Baldwin claims "robbed George for a moment of his last ray of intellect." People are equally helpless at defending themselves against William Mitten's handsomeness, and because of their good looks, neither Evelina nor William ever has to earn the love or respect of others, as Longstreet suggests; they become self-centered, lazy, and vapid. The need for discipline, austerity in child raising, and thrift were obsessive concerns of Longstreet and a sacred trust of the female characters in his stories. When a woman exerts the proper kind of authority and demonstrates plain virtues, she is extolled as "the most lovely of women." When she values physical beauty, current fashions in music, literature, or clothing, or when she looks to Philadelphia or the urban East for moral guidance, she brings ruin to her husband and children. Perhaps Longstreet justified the patriarchal domination of his own home by revealing the precarious existence of families run by headstrong women. We guess that Evelina is one of a new breed of Georgia women greatly distrusted by the author.

At the beginning of "The Charming Creature," Baldwin catalogs qualities he has observed in his nephew George's mother. Though he is a bachelor, indicating that few women have measured up to the standards of his sister-in-law, his composite list of attributes has a tone of sincerity which suggests Longstreet took such qualities very seriously; Mrs. Baldwin is "pious but not austere, cheerful, but not light, generous, but not prodigal; economical, but not close; hospitable, but not extravagant" (82). One of her most noteworthy qualities is her sense of self-discipline and organization. She knows how to keep all the members of her household, children and servants, "everything . . . with perfect system" (83). Longstreet, John Pendleton Kennedy, William Gilmore Simms, Thomas Nelson Page, and especially William Faulkner (in *The Unvanquished,* for example) depict similar heroic southern gentlewomen, soft-spoken but supremely capable and courageous. George Bagby's description of the antebellum matron, written in 1877, provides the southern ideal of womanhood which so many of these authors have sentimentalized:

The ways of the great world had ceased, long ago, to be her ways. She lived in a little world of her own. She cared not to keep pace with the fast-changing fashions, which to her pure mind, were not always for the better. Her manner was not, in the usual sense, high-bred; for hers was the highest breeding, and she had no manner. But her welcome as you entered her door, and her greeting, meet her where you might, on the endless round of her duties, in-doors or out, was as simple and genial as sunshine, and sweet as spring water.[16]

Evelina Smith, unfortunately, shares few of these idealized qualities. She represents for Longstreet the undisciplined child of nouveau riche merchants, indulged and affected. Like many others who are satirized in *Georgia Scenes,* Evelina has been educated in Philadelphia, a city synonymous with pretentious, unprincipled behavior in the minds of Longstreet's narrators. She succeeds in concealing her shallowness from George long enough to trap him into marriage, for even an impassioned letter from his mother fails to dissuade George from his choice. And so Baldwin indicates that being impervious to parental counseling can be fatal. Within weeks of marriage George realizes that he has made a terrible mistake. Besides Evelina's general frivolousness, her chief flaw appears to be her failure to discipline the servants. This shortcoming George bears "in silence, but in anger" as he observes "their idleness, their insolence, and their disgusting familiarities with his wife." Evelina appears to shrink from the familiarities of some of George's friends, however, which occasions him to comment: "You are certainly the strangest being that I ever met with; you are more respectful to negroes than whites" (105). Evelina's permissive attitudes toward her servants must have shocked the readers of Baldwin's narrative, just as George's racial attitudes are distasteful to a modern reader.

What is surprising in the narrative is the swift disintegration of the bridegroom into an alcoholic. Following a delayed supper for his lawyer friends, George bursts into a fury at his wife which "revolutionized" his whole character. He becomes severely depressed and begins "to surrender himself to the bottle" (108). When Evelina's father loses his fortune, she temporarily becomes dependent on George and mends her ways; but soon she loses her resolve to become a domestic paragon and "George . . . surrendered himself to drink and to despair and died the drunkard's death" (109). Baldwin concludes his tale with a warning to mothers "against bringing up their daughters to be 'charming creatures,' " reflecting the fears of even antebellum authors that unchecked permissiveness will wreck the moral order of the world.

Although Baldwin emerges in *Georgia Scenes* as a critic of newly rich, would-be sophisticates, he confines himself to general social issues. Hall, on the other hand, is willing to involve himself in specifically political satire. Leaving the domestic tragedy and genteel trappings that Baldwin describes in "The Charming Creature," *Georgia Scenes* again switches to a simple rural setting where the rivalries of small towns are the subject of Hall's discursiveness in what may possibly be an early parable of states rights. "The Gander Pulling," published originally in the *Southern Recorder* on 15 January 1834, discusses the relationship of four Georgia towns, Augusta, Springfield, Harrisburg, and Cambelton. Hall implies that the desire of the last two to become united "in a single town, for the maintenance of those principles which they deemed essential to the public welfare" is naive; and the reader is not surprised that the author who published the *States Right Sentinel* should show more respect toward Springfield, which "espoused the States Rights creed." The narrator explains:

Instead of the towns of the several states getting into *single bodies* to preserve the *public welfare,* her doctrine [Springfield's] was, that they should be kept in *separate bodies* to preserve the *private welfare.* She admitted frankly, that, living, as she always had lived, right amid gullies, vapours, fogs, creeks, and lagoons, she was wholly incapable of comprehending that expansive kind of benevolence, which taught her to love people whom she knew nothing about, as much as her next door neighbors. (111)

The description of the gander pulling that follows elaborately develops small-town rivalries, making victory in the contest a matter of community pride. When, however, Fat John Folger triumphs in pulling off the greased gander's head, all but one countryman responds good-naturedly to his success, and even he, according to Hall, is reconciled following "a pretty little piney-woods fight." Furthermore, John spends his winnings on drinks for all the participants. Therefore it appears that small communities can solve their own differences in their own way without outside interference, and that people respond more naturally to neighbors in specific incidents than to abstract conceptions of community, enforced by the federal government. Naturally, the main interest in "The Gander Pulling" is the somewhat sickening picture of a popular local amusement, but this story captured the interest of both William Gilmore Simms and Edgar Allan Poe, the latter considering it a "gem," worthy, in every respect, of the writer of "The Fight" and "The Horse-Swap."

The original publication date of the next story, "The Ball," was once thought to be 1832, but James Scafidel has noted its appearance in the *States Rights Sentinel* on 6 March 1834. Baldwin's tone in "The Ball" is mock-refined, and the society chatter of his narrative makes a startling contrast to the earthiness of "The Gander-Pulling." Although the reader is expected to smile tolerantly at the coarse country pleasures in Hall's tale, he is also expected to join Baldwin in some disdainful head shaking at the decadence of urban pastimes. Baldwin's basic comic technique is to place characters who disregard the conventions of polite society in the midst of a pretentious gathering. Deflating those who have assumed airs then becomes the main source of the reader's pleasure and central focus of the author's moral. Thus, in "The Ball" the graceless and rough-speaking Mr. Crouch manages to offend nearly every elegant lady at the party, mixing up their dance cards and muttering tactless remarks. American playwrights in Longstreet's day and later frequently employed a similar technique in their comedies. For example, Anna Cora Mowatt's *Fashion* enjoyed great popularity from the time of its opening in New York in 1842 until its appearance in other cities in the last part of the century by contrasting the rough mannerisms of its hero with the deceitful affectations of the society people who try to exploit him. In post–Civil War local color fiction, there are countless good-hearted country bumpkins whose crude honesty is despised by urban snobs.

In the South, Thomas Nelson Page would some years later attempt to satirize upper-class people who had forsaken simple but patrician values for the world of fashion. Page's satirical portraits in *Gordon Keith* (1903) and *John Marvel, Assistant* (1909) are both entertaining and authentic, befitting an aristocratic Virginian who possessed sufficient social finesse to become ambassador to Italy. Page perceived the flaws of the beau monde, but he admired the wit and luxury of the salons in great cities, with the result that his fashionable characters are interesting as well as vain.

Beyond a certain point, Longstreet had little patience with elegant gatherings and was especially ill at ease with bright, socially aggressive women. His portraits of such occasions are not so much satires of the jaded as they are slapstick put-downs of truly ridiculous people. He does, however, provide a clever description of modern ballroom dancing as it appears to an old-timer:

> The dancing of the ladies was, with few exceptions, much after the same fashion. I found not the least difficulty in resolving it into the three motions of a turkey-cock strutting, a sparrow-hawk lighting, and a duck walking. Let the reader suppose a lady beginning a strut at her own place, and ending it (precisely as does the turkey-cock) three feet nearer the gentleman opposite her; then giving three sparrow-hawk bobs, and then waddling back to her place like a duck, and he will have a pretty correct idea of their dancing. Not that the three movements were blended at every turn of the dance, but that one or more of the three answered to every turn. The strut prevailed most in balancing; the bobs, when balanced to; and the waddle, when going round. To all this Mrs. Mushy was an exception. When she danced, every particle of her danced, in spite of herself.
>
> There was as little variety in the gentlemen's dancing as there was in the ladies'. Any one who has seen a gentleman clean mud off his shoes on a door mat, has seen nearly all of it; the principal difference being, that some scraped with the pull of the foot, some with a push, and some with both. (128)

In "The Ball," Baldwin vacillates between pomposity and puerility in denouncing Georgia society matrons. Although their names, Mrs. Mushy, Miss Rino, Miss Gilt, suggest the stereotyping of Restoration dramatists, Baldwin's women lack the comic vitality and humanity we associate with an Etheridge or a Wycherly. The picture of newly rich Georgia husbands preferring a back-room game of cards to promenading in the ballroom is potentially fine material for social history, but Baldwin never exploits it, preferring to focus on jejeune debutantes whose tardiness at keeping their social appointments and whose immodesty, indicated by their preference for the waltz, lead to duels and near tragedy. It is hard to understand how a man who appears to have had close, satisfying relationships with his wife and daughters, all sensible, intelligent women who led exemplary lives, could portray their sex so unflatteringly, unless his bias were actually a pose, a part of his writer's mask. Whatever his motives may have been, his portraits of women lack the believability of his male characters.

Baldwin returns as the storyteller in "The Mother and Her Child," a three-and-a-half-page sketch which first appeared in the *States Rights Sentinel* on 2 June 1834. As in "The Ball," "The Song," "The Charming Creature," and other accounts of the new Georgians distrusted by Longstreet and his narrators, he again suggests that permissiveness is the source of vanity and self-indulgence. Such permissiveness and coddling in the home are viewed as the primary threats to strong character development. In "The Mother and Her Child," a mother and black nursemaid exhaust themselves in attempting to discover why an eight-month-old baby is crying, while Baldwin imitates their exaggerated baby-talk and cooing. The child-centered home, catering to infants' and children's whims, is continually singled out in Longstreet's work as the origin of social decay. Baldwin's heavy-handed rendition of the mother's baby talk is more tedious than amusing, but the most offensive aspect of the story is the mother's rude, even brutal treatment of her servant, which appears to amuse rather than appall Baldwin. Interestingly, phrases, such as "You lie, you slut," which the mother hurls at the black girl would never appear in tidewater fiction and suggest that rich young Georgia matrons were considerably less refined than their Virginia counterparts.

The faults of contemporary Georgia are temporarily forgotten in the next story, which retreats several decades into Longstreet's boyhood. "The Debating Society," first published in the *States Rights Sentinel* on 5 March 1835, begins with an authorial intrusion stating that "the following is not strictly a 'Georgia Scene'; but as Georgians were the chief actors in it, it may perhaps be introduced with propriety into these sketches." Unlike the other sketches, this one is primarily an autobiographical anecdote concerning the antics of Longstreet and his school chum

McDuffie (here thinly disguised as Longworth and McDermont) at Waddel's Academy, and the author's apologetic opening sentence appears to challenge his right to appear personally in the *Scenes,* even if he, too, is a native Georgian. His experiment succeeds because the aesthetic distance between the educated narrator and his characters in the rest of *Georgia Scenes* is here maintained, obviously not by differences in social class between the author and his subject, but by contrasts between the Judge's stately behavior in maturity and the reckless exuberance and fondness for pranks he associates with lost youth.

"The Debating Society" is also unique in *Georgia Scenes* in that it is a story about two highly educated boys, Longworth and McDermont. All the story's humor depends on sophisticated word play and verbal skills comprehensible only to an educated reader. In fact, some knowledge of legal jargon is requisite for complete appreciation. The two high-spirited young men, known as imperious debaters "more from uncommon volubility than from any superior gifts or acquirements," decide to practice a hoax on their fellow students by imposing a subject on their debating society which makes no sense at all. The topic they choose is "whether at public elections, should the votes of faction predominate by internal suggestions or the bias of jurisprudence." The result is a witty parody of legal jargon, debating rhetoric, and youthful imagination and is based very probably on an actual event in the author's youth. In the story Longworth defends "internal suggestion" and McDermont "bias of jurisprudence." The former raises such nonissues as "Are there any innate maxims?" and adds that "with that subject and this there is such an affinity, that it is impossible to disunite them, without prostrating the vital energies of both, and introducing the wildest disorder and confusion, where, by the very nature of things, there exists the most harmonious coincidences and the most happy and euphoric congruities" (137).

McDermont, challenging his friend, urges the audience "to distinguish true eloquence from the wild ravings of an unbridled imagination" and, of course, follows with ravings of his own that "faction in all its forms is hideous" and that followers of Longworth's proposal will be the victims of "thieves," "robbers," and "murderers." Longstreet's early forensic training, as well as his experience with courtroom legal tactics and his later contact with the bombast of sermons and religious debates, developed in him a keen ear for both the vapid and the hysterical phrase.

Poe called "The Debating Society" the "best thing in the book—and indeed one among the best things of the kind we have ever read."[17] Despite disagreements as to its comic merits, the sketch effectively confirms the Judge's alertness to verbal nuances and generally preserves a high quality of wit and entertainment.

"The Militia Company Drill" introduces a third narrator into *Georgia Scenes,* Timothy Crabshaw. As Longstreet comments in his note to the reader, the story was not his own but written by a friend some twenty years before the publication of the book. The friend has been identified by Richard H. Clark in his *Memoirs,* and by Wade in his biography of Longstreet, as Oliver Hillhouse Prince. Prince came to Georgia at the end of the eighteenth century and was admitted to the Georgia bar in 1806. He was a U. S. senator, the author of *Digest of Georgia Laws* (1822), and a trustee of the university at Athens.

Perhaps Longstreet published "The Militia Company Drill" out of respect for Prince or as a debt of friendship. Why the name Timothy Crabshaw was selected as a pseudonym is not known. Poe and other nineteenth-century southern critics have attested to the popularity of such stories about military drills in the 1830s, and Bert Hitchcock, in a recent biography of Richard Malcolm Johnston, notes Johnston's use of similar subject matter in "The Various Languages of Billy Moon," which was collected in the author's *Dukesborough Tales* (1871). Hitchcock concluded that Johnston's story reflected his "combative pride," a characteristic of his middle Georgian boyhood, and added that "making use of the formal fights which were the highlight of militia muster days . . . is once more closer to the older humorists, most notably to A. B. Longstreet." Poe insisted the Crabshaw version was without "equal . . . in the matter of broad farce,"[18] and Davidson called it "irresistibly amusing."[19] Few modern readers would agree with their judgment. The story seems needlessly detailed, pointless, and confusing. Captain Clodpole, the militia leader, gives contradictory instructions, bellows at his men, and eventually precipitates chaos by ordering a platoon wheeling movement that sends all his soldiers scurrying in different directions. Perhaps the farce could succeed as a one-act play since the effect depends on the ability to visualize the discomfort, bewilderment, and blundering of the officer and his men.

This story, like "The Debating Society," interrupts the pattern of rural-urban contrasts that prevailed in the earlier stories; both works may also draw on Longstreet's recall of personal experiences, as a schoolboy exercising his debating skills and as the captain of the 398th Company of the Georgia militia. Longstreet may have placed them in the middle of his book to temper the emerging moral bias of the collected sketches; his avowed purpose was to entertain, and he may have worried that a rather insistent didactic tone was developing in the Hall and Baldwin tale swapping. "The Militia Company Drill" became an odd cause célèbre among Longstreet's reading public, for Thomas Hardy appears to have copied either it, or a similar earlier sketch by Prince, in his 1880 edition of *Trumpet Major.* It is a comment on the curious taste of the era that there should be readers on two continents eager to enjoy these repetitious tales of military practice maneuvers.

In "The Turf," Hall describes a horse race that he attends with his friend Baldwin, marking the first occasion when both narrators appear together. This was originally a *Southern Recorder* story, appearing on 20 November 1833. All levels of Georgia society are present at the race, as Hall's description indicates:

Crowds of persons, of all ages, sexes, conditions, and complexions, were seen moving toward the booths; some on foot, some on horseback, some in gigs, some in carriages, some in carts, and some in wagons. The carriages (generally filled with well-dressed ladies) arranged themselves about thirty or forty paces from the starting-point, toward the centre of the turf. Around these circled many young gentlemen, each riding his prettiest, whipping, spurring, and curbing his horse into the most engaging antics, and giving visible token that he thought every eye from the carriages was on him, and every heart overpowered by his horsemanship. (152)

While racing was an extremely popular sport and attracted even the most pious elements of society, Longstreet himself followed the example of his mentor, Dr. Waddel, who strongly disapproved of the sport. This disapproval had some sectarian overtones since the Episcopalians held their state convention during race week to ensure a quorum, whereas the Presbyterians, led by Dr. Waddel, were generally censorious of any gambling activities. Nevertheless, Hall's account, while disapproving, treats more the humorous aspects of the sport than the sordid experiences Waddel had related in *Memoirs of the Life of Caroline Elizabeth Smelt* (1819). Many of Hall's criticisms seem reasonable and just. For example, he notes that he saw "Major Close, who two hours before declared he had not enough to pay a poor woman for the making of the vest he had on, treat a large company to a dollar bowl of punch . . . and stake fifty dollars on a race." Another gentleman wagering fifty dollars had "four days before permitted his endorser to lift his note in bank for one hundred dollars" (153). The desperation of gamblers, already hopelessly in debt, to redeem their losses with "one big win" is a timeworn theme, but Longstreet was intrigued with neurotic obsessions and, as will be seen in *William Mitten,* was not insensitive to the dilemma of a divided or tormented personality. The central didactic purpose in "The Turf" is to suggest that a gambler at the racetrack loses all perspective on life except the immediate game and that there is a general suspension of good judgment in the habitués of the track. Hall notes that men who never drank liquor in other situations become heavy drinkers at the races. And there is a disruption of moral priorities among the spectators, so that the death of one of the jockeys in a race is considered a "little accident" in an otherwise "delightful" experience.

"The Turf" also provides Hall with the opportunity to vent his paternalistic feelings about Negroes. "Uppity" black people are as offensive to him as are whites who feel no responsibility toward the humbler Negroes. A certain plantation ideal of each man in his place is implied. Nevertheless, the tone of "The Turf" is reasonably lighthearted. The sense of a festive occasion is conveyed effectively as is the narrator's amused bewilderment at the undisciplined and slightly hysterical crowds. Whimsical human nature is the subject of satire here rather than the dark social forces leading good Georgians away from the old values, as it is in many of the other stories.

The flawed nature of man is again the theme of "An Interest-

ing Interview" from the *Southern Recorder* in 1834, although
Hall as narrator expresses a limited faith in the doctrine of
perfectibility. Alcoholism is the subject of this sketch, and signifi-
cantly we are shown its dire effects on simple country people
who jeopardize their health and prospects for advancement by
taking solace in drink. Alcohol abuse among the affluent is not
an issue with Hall, who predicts that "in the higher walks of
life at least, if not from all grades of society" drinking will be
abandoned within "ten years more." Though some in the twentieth century consider excessive drinking a major factor in the
urban malaise, Hall suggests that in nineteenth-century Georgia
lonely, hardworking rural people are more susceptible to intem-
perance. Hall suggests that the "vice" of drinking, like so many
others, could be overcome with self-discipline and moral guidance, and he and Longstreet's other chief narrator, Baldwin,
epitomize the gentleman free from the vice.

Boisterous fun was acceptable to Longstreet, and his narrators
approvingly nod at the activities of gander pulling, boasting,
and practical jokes, but there is stern disapproval of jealousy,
lying, cheating, drinking, and gambling in his works. When
such vices surface, they are traced to lack of parental supervision
or the ignorance of established values, almost never to an individual's innate depravity. (Ransy Sniffle may be an exception
here, yet even he has been partially corrupted by his diet of
berries and dirt. Besides, as Merrill Maguire Skaggs has recently
pointed out, "Sniffle is considered inferior to all the other
townsfolk."[20]) The author's point of view makes an interesting
contrast to the Puritans' characterization of man as a basically
worthless creature easily tempted by the devil and, more frequently than not, eternally damned. Even after Longstreet converted to Methodism, which increased his awareness of sin and
his ardor for repentance, he retained a kind of Jeffersonian optimism about man's potential.

The humor of "An Interesting Interview" depends on the
non sequiturs of two inebriates whose pointless arguing delays
them until that they are drenched in a rainstorm. It is difficult
to extract comedy from such a situation, and Longstreet fares
no better than contemporary writers who exploit a drunk scene
for laughs. The pleas of little Billy Swift to his debased, alcoholic
father add pathos to the situation and make it even more distaste-

ful. Inconsistency of tone is perhaps the story's chief flaw. One cannot ridicule excessive drinking or show its degrading effects and simultaneously amuse readers with yet another tale of rough but harmless country pastimes.

"The Fox Hunt," printed first on 12 February 1835 in the *States Rights Sentinel,* offers Hall another opportunity for gentle self-satire and adds to the reader's overall impression that as a narrator Hall is less pretentious and more spirited than Baldwin. Whereas Longstreet alternated narrators frequently in the first half of *Georgia Scenes,* Hall's voice predominates in the second half, giving him a total of eleven, or nearly two-thirds of the "signed" sketches.

As we have seen, Hall is identified more with rural Georgia life and with primarily masculine activities. Longstreet himself, more comfortable with rough, open behavior than with sophisticated urban rituals, may have recognized the superiority of Hall's narratives. In any event, Hall dominates the concluding chapters of *Georgia Scenes* with boisterous, high action stories, leaving only "A Sage Conversation" for Baldwin to recount. The workmanship of the tales is increasingly haphazard, and one feels impatient at times with some rather obvious padding. The repetition of Somerville's "Chase" in its entirety in order to set the mood for the "Fox Hunt" is a good example of indiscriminate use of literary allusion. Fortunately, Hall soon comes to center stage as a somewhat clownish but appealing amateur hunter, blundering his way through a country weekend with attempted great style.

To begin with, he has difficulty sounding the hunter's horn properly, so that the noise accidentally reverberates throughout his rooming house, terrifying the landlord and his wife out of their sleep. Later he offers a wry judgment on the morning's activities: "I can't see what any man of common sense wants to be getting up this time of night for, in such cold weather, just to hear dogs run a fox" (168). The remaining events in the story tend to prove correct the landlady's assumption that fox hunting makes very little sense and that the hunter is essentially a comic figure. Even Hall's rapturous response to nature is couched in a classical rhetoric that reminds us this gentleman seldom rises from bed early in the morning: " 'Oh,' exclaimed I, 'how much, how beautiful, how glorious the firmament. . . .

I was lost in admiration of the splendors which surrounded me'" (169). His reverie is interrupted by a servant who leads him to his horse, "old Smooth Tooth."

Hall depicts himself as a kind of victim—of his own pride and folly in attempting the chase, of a glittering and seductive winter morning in which he nearly freezes, of his friends who have given him the oldest horse and scorn his ineptness. It requires a certain detachment in a society that prizes equitation above most other skills for Hall to reveal his inadequacies. He finds his tired old nag virtually unmanageable. His initial exhilaration at the first breath of morning air turns to despair as he finds himself freezing. The rapidity with which he moves from enthusiasm to discouragement attests to his superficial dedication to the sport. In one scene he parodies Absalom's fate by nearly hanging himself on a grapevine—surely the Biblical allusion was not lost on the audience of *Georgia Scenes.* None of the terminology of the chase is familiar to Hall, and he commits numerous faux pas. Soon after the fox nearly runs into Hall and Smooth Tooth, another hunter questions him:

> "Did you see him," exclaimed he, finding me near the trail.
> "Yes," said I distinctly.
> "How was his tail?"
> "I didn't notice particularly but sticking to him, I believe."
> "Oh, nonsense," said Crocket, "was his brush up or down?"
> "Neither," said I, "he *brushed* right across." (178)

This and other examples of self-effacing dialogue, along with the absence of didacticism or smugness, make "The Fox Hunt" one of the most lively and appealing stories in *Georgia Scenes.*

"The Wax-Works" is not so amusing as "Fox Hunt," but it is a harmless sketch about the antics of some middle-aged practical jokers who impersonate wax figures in a museum exhibit. Published first in the *States Rights Sentinel* on 19 February 1835, "The Wax-Works" derives part of its humor from the unflattering description of the participants. Fat Bill Grossly poses as a rotund Englishman, a drunkard named Pleasant Halgroce disguises his red face to pretend he's a corpse, and broad-faced Freedom Lazenby depicts Sleeping Beauty. The character of Lazenby was allegedly based on a lawyer friend of Longstreet's named Freeman Walker, but his personality is not distinguished from the others. Naive visitors to the wax-works declare it is almost impossible to distinguish the exhibits from "live folks" and Sleeping Beauty is judged "monstrous pretty." The impersonators refrain from laughter, but Bill Grossly is unable to resist biting a finger that prods his fat cheek. Thus exposed, the pretenders flee in high spirits from the angry mob. Hall is the narrator of this story, which is a kind of "filler" in *Georgia Scenes* and not particularly "Georgian" or even southern.

Baldwin narrates "A Sage Conversation," which deals with the comic gullibility of simple country women at the mercy of Ned Brace's practical jokes. Somewhat apologetically, Baldwin explains that although he is incapable of ridiculing "the aged matrons of our land," Ned Brace enjoys nothing better. While he and Baldwin are paying guests at a farmhouse, he solemnly comments to the old ladies who live there that he knew two men, George Scott and David Snow, who "became so much attached to each other that they actually got married," and adds: "And they raised a lively parcel of children; as fine a set as I ever saw, except their youngest son, Billy: he was a little wild, but, upon the whole, a right clever boy himself" (188).

The irrelevant reference to wild little Billy is in the best tradition of humorous writing and compares with the loose, anecdotal discourse of young Huckleberry Finn. The ladies are too stunned to demand clarification immediately, but they brood over the odd situation during their evening chat before the fire while Brace and Baldwin are pretending to sleep in an adjoining room. These women gossip as much as the ladies in town, but their talk lacks the spitefulness and sham of the drawing-room chatter Baldwin despises. When they wake the next morning, they courageously require an explanation from Brace about the bizarre Scott-Snow union. He replies that they were both widowers with children "before they fell in love with each other and got married." One of the elderly women comments, "The lackaday! I wonder none of us thought o' that," which is another good example of comic understatement, especially when we realize that the homosexual implications of Ned's story have been circumvented.

The mixture of the ungrammatical speech and stoic dignity of the old women with the combined rakishness and patronizing kindness of the urban paying guest contributes to a subtle human exchange in "A Sage Conversation" and makes it an appropriate concluding sketch for Baldwin.

Hall's final sketch in the collected tales is the boisterous "Shooting-Match." Its original publication place and date have been lost. As in "The Fox Hunt," the comedy depends upon Hall's discomfort at being required to perform athletic feats unsuited to a man of his age and ability. And as in the earlier story, he unexpectedly succeeds where superior competitors fail. "Shooting-Matches are probably nearly coeval with the colonization of Georgia," Hall explains, adding that "they are not as common as they were twenty-five or thirty years ago" (197). As the story first appeared in the *States Rights Sentinel* in February of 1835, the heyday of the shooting-match as sport appears to have been the first decade of the new century. Hall is drawn into the match by "a swarthy, bright-eyed, smerkly little fellow," a "cracker" named Billy Curlew from one of the northeastern counties, who carried a rifle that dated from the War of 1812. At first the two strangers exchange good-natured insults, and Hall comments, "I knew my man and knew what kind of conversation would please him most" (198). The ritualistic put-downs and jokes must have amused earlier readers on their own merits. They are no longer "side-splitting," perhaps, but they add an authentic regional flavor to the tale and an historical perspective. The prize in the shooting-match is a side of beef divided for the five best shots. Hall, who is hardly able to lift "Soap Stick," the rifle he borrows from Curlew, by sheer accident makes the second-best shot, leading the group to assume that his "wabbling" of the piece had been intentional. He has therefore defended his masculinity and his dignity. Hall speaks of Curlew and his friends affectionately, mocking his own inadequacies and blind good luck.

Curlew, who originally assumed that Hall was running for political office and was merely currying favor by taking part in the match, reassures the stranger that he has proved his worth. The rest of the group are equally ready to express their friendly acceptance of an outsider, and Hall comments:

As I turned to depart, "Stop a minute, stranger!" said one: then lowering his voice to a confidential but distinctly audible tone, "What you offering for?" continued he. I assured him I was not a candidate for anything; that I had accidentally fallen in with Billy Curlew, who begged me to come with him to the shooting-match, and, as it lay right on my road, I had stopped. "Oh," said he, with a conciliatory nod, "if you're up for anything, you needn't be mealy-mouthed about it 'fore us boys; for we'll all go in for you here up to the handle."

"Yes," said Billy, "dang old Roper if we don't go our death for you, no matter who offers. If ever you come out for anything, Lyman, jist let the boys of Upper Hogthief know it, and they'll go for you to the hilt, against creation, tit or no tit, that's the *tatur*." (214)

Thanking the group, Hall affirms his position as a man who has grown beyond simple country folk but who continues to interact with them and respect their ways and who is comfortable when they call him by his first name.

Thus, *Georgia Scenes* concludes with a restatement of the author's predominant themes—the need for educated men to check prideful tendencies through contact with unlettered, simple people and the need to synthesize the frontier spirit of Georgia's past with the more sophisticated culture evolving in the nineteenth century.

Chapter Three

The Legacy of
Georgia Scenes

The immediate success that followed the publication of *Georgia Scenes* far exceeded the author's expectations of popularity and initiated a series of literary influences that have continued to the present day. Beyond Milledgeville and Augusta, where the individual sketches had first appeared, other southerners began referring to the Judge as "the great Longstreet," a title repeated by the editors of the *Southern Literary Messenger.*[1] At South Carolina College, Professor Maximilian Laborde insisted that the *Scenes* were "perfect, and thousands among us bear witness to their exact fidelity, nor have we been without a personal observation which would give us some right to pass a judgment upon them."[2] Poe, as has been noted, praised many of the book's individual sketches, and he concluded his enthusiastic review for the *Messenger* by calling the *Scenes* a "very humorous, and very clever book."[3] Methodist Bishop Oscar P. Fitzgerald's assessment was also important since his biography of the author provided the first sustained critical treatment of his work. He commented:

The fidelity of these sketches to nature is recognized by every reader who has any knowledge of the people of whom and of which he wrote. . . . On their first appearance they were recognized as masterpieces of their kind, and thousands of Georgia homes re-echoed with the mirth they provoked. The sketches were written at an age when all enjoyment is most intense, and the intense zest of the writer is caught by the reader. In [some of the] sketches you almost hear the laughter of the crowd at the broader passages of coarse, rollicking fun while you see the smile that plays over the features of the author in the lighter and subtler touches that now and then give a special charm to his page. True humor is never wholly separated from genuine pathos, and there are pathetic touches in *Georgia Scenes* that go straight to the heart.

The dialect is perfectly rendered—a dialect that yet lingers in some parts of rural Georgia. The dialogue exhibits the perfect art that conceals art. The dramatic instinct was possessed by Judge Longstreet in no small degree. Every character he sketches is consistent with itself.

. . . It is safe to predict that the *Georgia Scenes* will be laughed over in the homes of our people long after many a more pretentious book now popular shall have sunk beneath the sluggish waters of the sea of oblivion.[4]

Georgia Scenes was, indeed, instantly successful. In 1844, six years after the first edition of *Georgia Scenes* had been printed, Yale University conferred an honorary degree on Longstreet, indicating the extent to which the author's literary reputation had been recognized in northern literary circles. Frequent reprintings of the work attest to its admirable sales record, although actual sales statistics are unavailable. The first edition had been succeeded by eight additional printings in 1842, 1846, 1850, 1854, 1857, 1858, 1860, and 1884, all appearing under the rubric of "second edition." A third edition, referred to as "a new edition from plates," appeared in 1897 and an edition was also published in Atlanta in 1894. Davidson's generous assessment of the volume in 1869 has already been discussed, and George M. Hyde writing for the *Bookman* in 1897 declared that "A. B. Longstreet's *Georgia Scenes* marked the beginning of literary realism in the United States and is American Humor writ large."[5]

Contributions to the *Mirror*

When the first edition of the *Scenes* appeared, Judge Longstreet was nearing fifty; he was well known as a lawyer-politician and was the friend of Calhoun and McDuffie. The next thirty years found him increasingly involved in the area of morality, an interest frequently expressed in the tales of *Georgia Scenes.*

After collecting his first stories for *Georgia Scenes,* he continued to write sketches, mostly at the request of friends or journal editors who wanted fresh southern materials, but without the enthusiasm that marked his earlier work. Prior to the second edition of *Georgia Scenes,* however, he turned out a few more stories, all written in a darker tone, politically conservative and sedate.

"Little Ben," drafted early in 1838, was published in his friend William Tappan Thompson's the *Mirror* that spring and was republished in the *Southern Literary Messenger* in June. Longstreet wrote a lengthy preface to the tale, which is actually a pair of sketches about hunting squirrels and catching catfish. It was no longer enough for him to spin a yarn; he had to frame his works with scholarly digressions, in this case, allusions to Horace's satires. Perhaps he was merely indulging a renewed interest in the classics. More likely, he was trying to attribute some intellectual significance to a very simple story and to assure his readers that Georgia's leading humorist was himself no cracker. In the first sketch, little Ben climbs a tree to fetch a squirrel but does not receive the reward he was promised. In the second, he overwhelms his cousin John by getting two huge catfish in the same day. Both stories are pointless to an absurd degree, although the author's defenders believe their charm depended entirely on their being read aloud by the Judge himself with his droll mimicry of little Ben's dialect and his perfect sense of comic timing.

During the same year, Longstreet wrote a "Family Picture" for the *Mirror.* In it he describes what he considers a rather typical upper-middle-class Georgia family. Undoubtedly, by 1838 there were many more prosperous and educated families in the villages or smaller cities than Longstreet would have seen as a small boy in Augusta. The Butlers, the author tells us, are "a fair specimen of Georgia family generally, at the heads of which are parents of good sense, morals, and well-improved minds."[6] The Butlers' family group is a microcosm of the kind of society Longstreet hoped would develop in the South.

The first part of the story satirizes abstract theories of child raising. As a young husband, Gilbert Butler believes that a father should never discipline a child incapable of distinguishing between right and wrong. His wife, Eliza, considers his principle reasonable but inapplicable to actual child-rearing. Although Gilbert is supported by his friend, the narrator of the story, Eliza's position is vindicated when some years later she prevents her young son from being seriously burned by spanking him.

The father's attempts to reason with the boy about the dangers of a candle have been futile. One suspects that Longstreet the disciplinarian has always been on the mother's side in matters of practical discipline, but his theory about raising children with firmness is better proved by having Eliza win two converts to her position. There is a certain charm in Longstreet's amused portrait of two intelligent, well-educated males piously applying textbook solutions to the upbringing of yet unborn children. Longstreet himself generally deferred to the female's superior judgment in domestic matters, and his loving but somewhat bemused fathers are among his more appealing stereotypes.

The second part of the story concentrates on Gilbert's and Eliza's children (in time, they had eight) when they have reached "the age of reason" (99). Longstreet's genuine love of family life is reflected in his description of its rituals, such as "hog-killing" on the old plantations. And he is obviously attracted to the mischievous child who is nevertheless basically moral and unswervingly loyal to his parents. His treatment of sibling rivalry is graphic but understanding, and he is equally sympathetic toward the inevitable daily anxieties faced by the mother of a large family. The children taunt each other with pigs' tails (given to them by the plantation Negroes) and steal biscuits out of one anothers' hands. The story's final sibling conflict involves little Billy's assertion that his brother Abraham doesn't pray long enough at bedtime. This distresses his mother more than any of the other crises in the story; but when she probes more deeply into Abraham's behavior, he tells her the part of his prayers he did, in fact, have time to say: "God bless my father and mother." With such a proper respect for the fourth commandment, the boy "shows he's got a good heart" and will suffer "no danger" (114). "Family Picture" portrays a generally cheerful, energetic, and prosperous domestic scene. The moral seems to be that, given love and firm guidance, children can subdue their wilder impulses and will grow to imitate their parents in responsibility and wisdom.

Longstreet's next fictional contribution for the *Mirror* appears to have been "Darby Anvil," which was reprinted in the *Southern Literary Messenger* in January of 1844 and in the appendix of Fitzgerald's Longstreet biography in 1891. Fitzgerald claimed that the story had not been previously published, but one assumes he meant it had not been printed in a volume. Fitz R. Longstreet, the author's nephew, renamed it "Darby the Politician" when he included it in *Stories with a Moral* in 1912. There is an almost antipopulist feeling in this tale of corrupt politics and public ignorance; Darby is "living proof" that an ignoramus can dupe the ordinary citizen. Longstreet's distrust of the low-born and uneducated was never more openly expressed.

Longstreet intended a touch of levity in the local blacksmith's last name—Anvil—and this creates a lighthearted tone early in the story. Later, when Darby becomes the archetypal crooked politician and has a demoralizing impact on the entire state legislature, that earlier levity seems out of place. "Darby Anvil" sounds too much like a blue-collar everyman, not enough like a solitary scoundrel. Longstreet would not consciously have denigrated a man because he was a blacksmith, but because he was an ignoramus. Not only the Judge but even the most enlightened mid-nineteenth-century readers would have thought it presumptuous for an uneducated man to seek office. Nevertheless, it is hard to be comfortable with the author's undisguised social bias, and Darby's legend overflows with references to "the prejudices and weaknesses of the common people." Darby's influence over others "of his own class" is also deplored (53). To show how Darby is completely unsuited for public office, Longstreet provides a lengthy comic description of his scarecrow-like apparel, a suit of mud-colored homespun, woven by his wife.

The unintentional effect of Longstreet's sartorial digression is to invoke sympathy for a basically contemptible opportunist. Darby's political opponents, Smith and Jones, are so pedantic as to make them hardly preferable to Darby. Smith secretly aligns himself with Anvil against Jones. What wins the election for Darby, however, is a last-minute accusation that he was a fugitive from the law in Virginia. There were, of course, many fugitives in every corner of America at this time as David Crockett notes in *The Narrative of the Life of David Crockett.* The disclosure of Darby's legal difficulties led the crowd to believe he was being persecuted on the eve of his election, which provided the additional public sympathy he needed for a victory at the polls.

Longstreet has little sympathy for Darby's supporters, who, learning their candidate was victorious, "ate, drank, sung vulgar songs, and told more vulgar stories until about one o'clock, when, they or some of them, stalked forth and with drum and fife and yells drove sleep from the village until the dawn" (84).

Darby's political career turns out to be disastrous, ended only by his bad debts and alcoholism. Longstreet concludes that in favoring a single unqualified man the irresponsible electorate created a continuing problem: "Encouraged by his [Darby's] success, worthless candidates sprung up in every county" (86). Rather than attempt to govern themselves, simple people ought to elect educated, well-trained persons of a higher class than themselves and thus discourage political ambitions in common folk. He comments, "Presumptuous ignorance should be reprimanded with fearless tongue, its sins should be proclaimed abroad in warning to the people, and all good men should unite their efforts to redeem a State entirely from such influence" (87).

With such an obvious distrust of democratic political processes it is no wonder that Longstreet in the unhappy aftermath of little Alfred's death relinquished politics and public service for the personal calling of the ministry. Although this calling would occupy most of his time during the next decade, in his infrequent leisure moments he managed some time for writing.

More Sketches

The Judge was besieged with offers to publish more articles and books. His Methodist friend, George Pierce, founded the *Southern Ladies' Book* with the help of P. C. Pendleton and announced in an early issue that Longstreet would be a future contributor, but the journal failed before the busy administrator completed any more sketches. Pendleton, however, moved to Savannah and began a new magazine called the *Magnolia, or Southern Monthly.* Despite the patronage of William Gilmore Simms, who agreed to become its editor, the periodical also failed after a year, lasting only long enough to publish three Longstreet stories. "Julia and Clarissa," "The Old Soldiers," and "The Gnatville Gem" appeared between 1842 and 1843. All had probably been drafted four or five years previously and all were later included in *Stories with a Moral.*

Pendleton and Simms originally published "Julia and Clarissa" in two consecutive issues of *Magnolia,* September and October 1842. Longstreet considered it material for a novel rather than a journal story as he noted almost apologetically in his magazine preface. And, in fact, Mrs. Carp, one of the principal characters in *William Mitten,* is first introduced here. Mrs. Carp and her daughter Julia contrive to marry off Julia's brother Osborn to an heiress named Clarissa Gage. Clarissa frustrates their plans by choosing Milton Fisher, a young lawyer, impoverished but with a fine character and high prospects. As Wade suggests, the courtship has an authentic ring, especially since the story was set in 1816 when Longstreet was a poor but promising lawyer and courting his wealthy bride-to-be. The author suggests that idle ladies with too much imagination can distort basically simple situations. The Carps nearly convince Clarissa that Osborne will commit suicide if she refuses him, and the whole village becomes embroiled in Clarissa's selection of a husband. Mrs. Carp is an affected person, a kind of Mrs. Malaprop who uses expressions like "rich as Creasy" (165), and she creates ill-feeling in the community and frustrations for her children. Eventually after Clarissa has married Mr. Fisher, Julia and Osborn both find suitable mates, implying that young people left to their own devices will choose wisely. Parental concern with the wealth and position of in-laws reveals an evolution in Georgia society that Longstreet deplored. He believed the new Georgia matron, freed from the burdensome existence of the pioneer woman, was tempted to discharge her energy in frivolous projects.

The author's second contribution to the *Magnolia* was "The Old Soldiers" which Simms featured in the March issue of 1843. Its theme is the need to respect the memories and past accomplishments of elderly people. The parable of the good Samaritan is also alluded to in this story since old John Taylor is walking on foot to his granddaughter's house and he is met by strangers with varying degrees of charity.

The principal characters in the tale are the old soldiers themselves, Taylor and Chavers, who are survivors of the Revolutionary War. The latter is contemptuous of his sons who fought in the War of 1812 which was "mere child's play" and lacked Tories and prison ships. As in classical comedy, the plot turns on mistaken identity, or more precisely, on an unknown identity.

Chavers and Taylor both served under a Captain Ryan and were captured by Tories and taken to prison ships. The old men are delighted to discuss the war since they can no longer find a younger audience to listen to their stories, stressing the loneliness of those who survive most of their contemporaries. The story's recognition scene occurs when Taylor tells how a fellow prisoner was holding a spoon which was divided in two by a lightning bolt. Chavers, of course, was the prisoner and he had preserved the spoon handle in a pine box, which he would open only on the Fourth of July. Thus the old men are reunited, and Chaver's tall tale of the war is vindicated. The frankly sentimental theme is balanced by a believable description of the elderly protagonists with their physical and mental limitations, crustiness and self-justification. "The Old Soldiers" is the kind of unpretentious folk yarn Longstreet handled with ease.

The third Longstreet story published in the June 1843 issue of *Magnolia* is a more ambitious undertaking. "The Gnatville Gem" has a complicated plot and deals with confusing political issues and the mechanics of publishing a small newspaper. Longstreet describes a Connecticut editor who inexplicably arrives in a Georgia community and announces his intention of beginning a newspaper. As his name, Asaph Doolittle, suggests, he is a lethargic fellow, unassertive and impractical. Although he was raised in a Federalist family, Asaph is easily persuaded to make his paper a voice of Jeffersonian democracy. Longstreet may be satirizing the superficial political commitments of affluent northeasterners, but not much is made of this theme in the story. Rather, Longstreet seems more to focus on the petty quarrels of the townspeople, the triviality of their interests, and the hopelessness of trying to educate the majority.

Although he was past fifty when he wrote this story, Longstreet achieved some of the playfulness of *Georgia Scenes;* and while the author's antipopulism is apparent, the mood of the piece is not essentially bitter. In this regard, it is useful to compare "The Gnatville Gem" with Mark Twain's "The Man That Corrupted Hadleyburg," published in 1899. The latter's story is one of its author's darkest works, claiming that greed and hypocrisy so pervade the American scene that not a single uncorrupted person can be found in Hadleyburg, which is presented as the archetypal American community. Mark Twain's dismal tale appears to be an allegory of original sin without the comfort of eventual salvation. Longstreet's story may flirt with the notion of universal corruptibility, but it ends with a religious revival which salvages the better instincts of the village.

Longstreet manages to inject many of his personal biases and stylistic characteristics into the tale. We immediately forecast the ultimate ruin of Doolittle, when we discover that women found him "fair to look upon" (12), for no handsome man is ever successful in a Longstreet story. Next we find that although the Jeffersonians in Gnatville are mindless in their liberalism (almost an ironic rebuke to Jefferson, himself, who believed the common man capable of rational behavior and noble sentiments), they are far superior to the Hamiltonians, who, particularly in the person of Asaph, are lazy, self-interested, and morally vacuous. Still, Longstreet shows a sense of political fairness when he notes there are only three Federalists in the village, suggesting blind conformity on the part of the other citizens; and he praises an unnamed editor of the *Augusta Herald* whom, in spite of Federalist political views, he calls "one of the shrewdest, most intelligent and satiric writers of his time" (22–23). The extreme hostility of the Jeffersonians toward their political opponents indicates their naiveté. For example, one of the early names proposed for Doolittle's paper was *The Scourge of Federalism.* Probably the Federalists' endorsement of the hated Alien and Sedition Laws intensified distrust of their party in mid-century Georgia. Suspicion toward strangers in small towns is teasingly alluded to when Billy Figs, a local bumpkin, suggests the townspeople ride Doolittle out of town on a rail. Here Longstreet satirizes Billy's droll ignorance and somewhat childish exuberance but never implies any true maliciousness of spirit or brutality.

The main appeal of the "Gnatville Gem" to readers of his own day was probably Longstreet's lighthearted parody of the small-town press. By describing the *Gem*'s foolish content, Longstreet was free to try out some of his own comic limericks and rustic humor. He and his readers were greatly attracted to the possibilities of fun in such an enterprise, and the barrage of insults delivered by the *Gnatville Gem* and its rival paper, the *Augusta Herald,* are in the best tradition of frontier humor putdowns.

The story contains one of the few passages written in the playful backcountry spirit of the early Longstreet sketches. In quoting the editor of the *Augusta Herald,* Longstreet offered a fine example of the rural Satirical style:

> We received from the Post Office yesterday, a neat little roll, which we doubted not was a joint remission from two or three of our subscribers. Having no immediate call for money (a rare thing with us by the way) we put it into our fob, where we suffered it to remain until called for. Going to market the next morning, a chicken cart drove up, and as chickens were in great demand, a general scramble for them ensued. We secured six, having in either hand three, and being unwilling to entrust any of them to empty hands, where there was such a yearning for these feathered bipeds, we requested the countryman to insert his fingers in our fob, and draw out a little bundle of change that he would find there. He did as directed, and judge what was our surprise upon seeing the bundle opened, to find a newspaper, entitled the *Gnatville Gem.* We offered it to the farmer for the six chickens; but he refused to take it. We told him we did not deal in jewelry, and therefore could not say exactly what this gem was worth, but we had no doubt it was very valuable, and had cost Mr. Jefferson a good deal of money; but that we would give it to him for one chicken. Whereupon he grew crusty, cursed the Gem and Mr. Jefferson, and told us if we didn't offer him something better than that little thumb-paper for his chickens, he'd ease us of them mighty quick. We therefore requested him to put the Gem in our hat, and his hand in our vest-pocket, where he would find a little jewelry that he would perhaps like better. (23–24)

Humor in the Augusta paper was not limited to the editorial columns. Puns on the name Doolittle frequently appeared in the paper. Another time the Augusta paper included an Irish joke about a worker named Paddy who chose a "jack-plane" and "drawing knife" as instruments to clear new ground. The ignorant Irishman was compared to the inexperienced lawyers, Moore and Jeeter, whose contributions to the Gnatville paper seemed equally ludicrous and inappropriate.

Feeling there was a spy in their camp, Jeeter in retaliation wrote a satire of a hard-drinking Gnatville judge whom he believed responsible for the *Herald* satire. Calling his article "A little receipt for making a big judge," he alludes to the judge's obesity and heavy drinking: "Go down to Goose Creek—catch a gander—put a quill in his mouth—blow him up until his middle parts hide his thighs—pour a half pint of old Jamaica into him—set himself on the bench, and call him Potgot, and he will make an excellent judge" (26).

Although Jeeter later regrets his verbal attack on the judge, the paper has already gone to press. An angered judge returns Jeeter's volley with one of his own: "Catch a pole-cat, stuff him with brass, and call him Cheater, and he will make an excellent lawyer" (27).

In addition to being a battleground for insult swapping, the *Gem* also provides space for a lovers' quarrel. Young Charles Quick, ignored by Laura Dobson, composes a poem about a haughty lady named Gaura Gobson who has made insulting remarks about lawyers. When the poem appears in the *Gem* the whole community is scandalized by its impropriety. Eventually there is a feud involving almost all the citizens of Gnatville. The *Gem* is blamed for the contentious atmosphere of the formerly peaceful village and Doolittle takes a few belongings and leaves town. All the barbed insults, scathing limericks, and resulting fistfights are worthy of vintage Longstreet yarns. Although a casual reader might not anticipate the religious revival, which at the conclusion is needed to restore civility to the squabbling townspeople, the injection of a religious theme is consistent with Longstreet's strong dedication to Methodism in the 1840s and later. The story may also be a parable of the role of the press in politics and the irresponsibility of most newspaper editors. Petty grievances rather than substantive issues would then seem to be the mainstay of journalism, and one might come to the conclusion that matters of government are best left in the hands of professional statesmen.

Two additional Longstreet stories were announced in the November 1842 issue of the *Magnolia* but never appeared in any subsequent issues. Wade holds that the subject matter may have been "too rakish." Possibly they were rough drafts which Longstreet never bothered to complete. But even if they did once exist in a finished form, they now appear to be lost. One was called "John Bull's Trip to the Gold Mines" and the other was "The India Rubber Story."

One factor in Longstreet's declining interest in authorship may have been his concern that he had been exploited by publishers and had received insufficient remuneration for his efforts. During this same year, he wrote James B. Longacre, a Methodist friend who had moved to Philadelphia, to complain about being underpaid by Harper's for the second edition of *Georgia Scenes.* He employed his friend to help him discover if the publishing firm had defrauded him.

I am strongly inclined to the opinion that I have been shamefully imposed upon by the Harpers of New York, and I wish to bespeak your aid in detecting them if I am right in my suspicions. Be assured that nothing that you do in the matter shall involve you in any difficulties. You may perhaps have heard of my literary bagatelle called the "Georgia Scenes." I published an edition of 3950 cadences in Augusta; which after paying all expences [*sic*], giving away about two hundred & fifty copies, and selling 600 at very reduced prices netted me about $1300—and all this without sending a single volume north of the Potomac. The Harpers, having, I supposed repeated calls for the work, proposed to me to issue a new edition with Illustrations, they taking the expenses, and we dividing the profits. I agreed to the proposition, and at the end of 14 months after the work was issued, I received yesterday the subjoined account, whereby it appears that the net profits of 2750 vols is $432.26, the one-half of which $216.13 fully to the Harpers. Now I think it next to impossible that any one as well versed in book making as the Harpers should have been anxious to put out a work, which they must have forseen would have paid them so poorly, upon an entire sale of the whole edition. You perceive by this annexed bill that the cost of the edition was nearly 50 cents per vol. and that sales are at 67½ cents—such profit is nothing to me. Now will you, my dear brother, if possible, ascertain at what price the Booksellers in Philadelphia got the work from the Harpers and give me names of the purchasers. Get a copy of the work if it is to be had in Philadelphia and tell me what the charges in Philadelphia would have been, compared with those in the annexed bill. In making these inquiries you may with truth say, that the author intends to issue a revised edition of the first volume, with another volume not yet published; and he desires to know the best terms which he can get the work put out.[7]

If Longacre wrote a response to the Judge's note, it has been lost. What is revealing in the Judge's letter is his suspicious attitude toward a New York publishing firm and his fear of being exploited or duped. It was at this time in his life also that the northern and southern branches of the Methodist church met in New York and divided over the slave controversy. His bitter experience at the conference had made him angry with nearly all Yankee enterprises. Longstreet himself may have been disillusioned with publishing, turning his mind to activities he considered more important than writing. His family, who always regretted his abandonment of his literary interests, however, continued to praise his amusing tales and urged him to write another collection of stories. Such a collection was not forthcoming in the Judge's lifetime but his nephew organized a posthumous edition of his shorter works which was published in 1912.

Fitz R. Longstreet's Collection

Stories with a Moral, as the volume was called, is a collection of sketches written a half-century earlier. Six had not been previously collected but all had appeared in Georgia gazettes and journals. To fill out the volume, early versions of several chapters of *William Mitten* were included as well as some of the more popular narratives from *Georgia Scenes.* The thematic connection of the pieces is the moral lesson or message each conveys. It is fair to say that Longstreet viewed all human experiences in moral terms and that by nature he tended to create parables out of ordinary daily events.

Although the stories were written at different junctures of Longstreet's life, many of them possess a weary and cynical tone. The energy and freshness of *Georgia Scenes* balanced the Judge's somewhat harsh conservatism, but there is a distinctly reactionary feeling to *Stories with a Moral.* Pettiness and grotesque foolishness among country people is ubiquitous. Democracy is endangered by an irresponsible electorate motivated by sentiment. Small-town people are gossips, fortune hunters, social climbers. Young mothers are overly permissive with their children and undermine their husbands' authority in the home. The press, the legal profession, the political arena, the educational system are subjects less of satire than of despair. Several of the works provide us with valuable social history, sharpening one's perception of Georgia life in Longstreet's day; but they share with the stories of the late local color movement a pervasive sentimentality, an authoritarian narrator, and an entrenched middle-class point of view. Only "The Village Editor" and "Darby the Politician" among these stories contain any of the crude, hearty Georgia crackers the author made famous before the war, since the editor of the new collection seems to have selected his materials to conform to the mood of a more genteel, conservative literary era.

The first of the *Stories with a Moral* is "The Village Editor," which had appeared sixty-two years earlier as "The Gnatville Gem" in the *Magnolia* and has already been discussed. For its "moral" the tale warns of the dangers of irresponsible journalism.

Sentiment, not humor, dominates the next story, which originally appeared in October 1842, again in the *Magnolia*. The lesson of "The Old Soldiers" is that one ought to respect the old, and cherish their reminiscences and private legends.

The third story, "Darby the Politician," was first published in William Thompson's *Mirror* as "Darby Anvil," and was later reprinted in the *Southern Literary Messenger* and in Fitzgerald's *Judge Longstreet* under the same title. By the 1840s Longstreet may have lost whatever hope he may once have held in the average person's ability to participate wisely in government, but he argued here for a responsible, informed electorate.

The next two sketches, "Family Government" and "A Family Picture," were both originally published under one title, "A Family Picture," in Thompson's *Mirror* in 1838. Later Robert Whythe published a condensed version of "A Family Picture" in the 26 January 1853 issue of the *Home Gazette*. Eventually it was separated into the two stories that appear in *Stories With a Moral*. Both works emphasize the need for discipline, harmony, and consistency in family management.

"The Old Women" is a one-page tribute to "the aged matrons of our land," immediately recognizable as the first page of "A Sage Conversation" in *Georgia Scenes,* the story in which Ned Brace tells of two bachelors who marry and have children. In that tale, the old women are as gossipy and foolishly credulous as they are "pious" and "benevolent," but the opening tribute softens what might otherwise be a blistering satire of ignorant country women. In *Stories with a Moral,* only the eulogy to the selflessness and generosity of Georgia women remains. The lesson is clear: a fulfilling life is a "life of good offices."

Fitz R. Longstreet may have placed "The Old Women" in his text in order to offset the satirical view of their society counterparts in "The Matchmaker" (formerly titled "Julia and Clarissa"), which follows and emphasizes the self-interest of mothers with marriageable daughters. Like "The Matchmaker," "A Charming Wife" also points to a crisis in family values. Originally it appeared as "The Charming Creature as Wife" in the *States Rights Sentinel* in 1834 and was included in *Georgia Scenes*. It reveals the tragic consequences of raising a young woman to be a charming ornament to society rather than a responsible person. "The Ball" is also borrowed from *Georgia Scenes*, although it was originally published in 1832 in the Milledgeville *Southern Recorder*. Woman's vanity and the affectations of society are again a central issue. The final selections in *Stories with a Moral* are two chapters covering various episodes in the life of *William Mitten*. Since that novel never attained the popularity of *Georgia Scenes*, Fitz R. Longstreet may have concluded that the majority of readers of *Stories* would consider it new and interesting material.

There may be no deliberate pattern to *Stories with a Moral* but there are logical points of division within the volume. The first three stories deal with simple rural people who are generally unruly and ignorant but capable of making a contribution when provided with dignified leadership and religious inspiration. The next three stories show a more ideal picture of Georgia life— a bounteous but unpretentious plantation existence based on time-honored principles; they resemble in some ways the plantation fiction of J. P. Kennedy or later of Thomas Nelson Page. Finally, the last five chapters in the book deal with the affluent Georgia of Longstreet's later years, which he found unproductive, decadent in some ways, and vulgar. Here higher and lower classes have mingled in a common love of money and comfort.

Stories with a Moral did not enhance Longstreet's literary reputation. Still it is proper that his name should have been recalled at the close of the era of the local colorists, a proper "eulogy" for one who helped pave the way for that later generation of southern writers. The title of the volume also provides an appropriate comment on his contribution. The Judge had always considered himself more of a moral guide or social historian than a storyteller.

Chapter Four

The Sad Tale of
William Mitten

In the decade following the publication of *Georgia Scenes,* while Longstreet continued to be a spokesman for Georgia nationally and to enjoy his role as elder statesman in education and religion, events were taking place in Mississippi that would soon affect his life. John Waddel, a son of the old headmaster whom Longstreet had eulogized in 1841, had settled in Mississippi a year before his father's death. First a farmer, then an educator, he had become by 1844 a member of the board of trustees of the infant University of Mississippi. He proposed the name of Longstreet to the other trustees as an excellent candidate for the university's first presidency. Then he and his friend Jacob Thompson wrote to the Judge at Emory and asked him if he would accept the position.

Longstreet was flattered that young Waddel thought so highly of him and was also gratified that his fame had spread as far south and west as Mississippi. There were few challenges left to him at Emory, and in fact the danger persisted that his administration, far from dynamic, might eventually be discredited, considering the continued scarcity of operating funds and Longstreet's growing disinterest in the position. After the initial excitement of a new opportunity he was seldom able to concentrate on a project or to follow through with the tedious details of a daily routine. Perhaps he believed that Mississippi as a secular institution would provide him with an opportunity for "missionary work" on behalf of the Methodist church. At least some trustees at Mississippi, concerned that, as president, Longstreet might try to impose his own religious views on the students, balked at young Waddel's nomination. Others pointed out that the Judge had never officially applied for the position.

Much to the embarrassment of young Waddel, the trustees refused to elect Longstreet and chose instead a man half the Judge's age. Thus, George Frederick Holmes, a Virginian who had been born in Georgetown, British Guiana, in 1820, became the university's first president, and Longstreet, who had already resigned from Emory, found himself in a virtual state of retirement. While the Longstreets had sufficient funds to permit a comfortable, even stylish retirement, the Judge's pride was deeply hurt by his "rejection," and he was embarrassed by his need to explain his sudden lack of employment to friends. Fortunately, Centenary College in Louisiana provided him with an unexpected opportunity to continue his career. Also a Methodist institution, Centenary was comparable in size and purpose to Emory, and its trustees, learning of the Judge's availability, unanimously elected him its president.

A New Presidency

Eager for a new project and anxious to save face, Longstreet moved to Jackson, Louisiana, in 1849 and began his new assignment. His term of office was to be short and unsatisfying—he later referred to his experience there as "the five most tormenting" months of his life.[1] Wade listed interfering widowed mothers as one major source of annoyance and a powerful system of student government as another. The rigid authoritarian particularly disapproved of a charter guaranteeing that students should share equally with the board of trustees the power of initiating legislation concerning school policy. The executive and judiciary branches of Centenary were controlled by the faculty. Longstreet would have preferred that the board of trustees frame all legislation and believed that he, rather than the faculty or students, should enforce the trustees' rulings. It appears to have been a classic problem of the delegation of power in academia and calls to mind the conflicts between college administrations and students of more recent years. Evidently, the "democracy" of Centenary was too entrenched to be threatened by the college's skeptical new president. Longstreet's frustrations at any rate found expression in his resumption of authorship, for, asked by two students to contribute to a literary magazine they had established in the village, he wrote the first five chapters of

Master William Mitten; or, A Youth of Brilliant Talents Who Was Ruined by Bad Luck, which were printed in weekly installments. Longstreet evidently sought vengeance on the permissive widows of Jackson, Louisiana, whose pampering of their sons had dismayed him, by portraying in these early chapters two especially foolish mothers whose indulgence leads directly to the ruin of their sons. Closely related to his disapproval of these matriarchs is his concurrent theme of the need for discipline and austerity in an academic community. That Longstreet believed the spirit of anarchy prevailed in a Methodist men's college in antebellum Louisiana suggests his views on education were anachronistic even in his own day. Fifty-eight years old now, the author was nostalgic for his own childhood and for an educational system he recalled as strict, wholesome, and just. He conjured up his past from an adult perspective, undoubtedly repressing much of the pain of growing up, siding now with the elders who had once passed judgment on him. Therefore, although most modern critics would later value the novel he was writing only as a social and historical document of the antebellum years, it would reveal many of the pedagogical methods of Georgia in the late eighteenth and early nineteenth centuries, when the author had acquired his own education.

A New Novel Appears

In *Southern Field and Fireside,* a new weekly periodical, *Master William Mitten; or, A Youth of Brilliant Talents Who Was Ruined by Bad Luck* was published serially between 28 May and 19 November of 1859. (It was later published in book form in Macon, Georgia, in 1864 and again in 1869.) *William Mitten* is part bildungsroman and part moral handbook. The author's purpose in writing the novel was avowedly didactic, and there are ample pauses in the narrative where Longstreet sums up the lessons that can be inferred from William's experiences. At such times Longstreet the college president can be heard, offering in a heavy-handed way the wisdom he has gleaned from observing young men throughout his academic career. Longstreet's self-assurance and consistency were perhaps his most important assets as an authority figure, and those same qualities provide this rather carelessly written novel with a workable point of view. He is both the omniscient narrator in *William Mitten* and also similar in character to William's uncle, Captain David Thompson, who is a kind of central consciousness through whom we learn much of William's early history. The usually charitable Wade has complained about the unfinished style and even the poor grammar of *William Mitten,* and the author himself was skeptical of its merit. He evidently never put his heart into the book nor considered it worth a final publishing or revision. But while *William Mitten* is technically inferior to much of *Georgia Scenes* and tedious in its sermonizing, it deserves recognition from scholars for two reasons: first, Longstreet attempts with some success to create believable characterizations rather than the caricatures that made him a famous writer; second, despite his moralizing and unsophisticated, discursive style, he reveals more of his personal attitudes and feelings in *William Mitten* than he does in *Georgia Scenes* and provides an especially convincing analysis of Georgia society.

The Longstreet of *Georgia Scenes* was a detached aristocrat, amused and sometimes touched by the lives of the frontiersmen. His experiences on the circuit court taught him to admire their vitality, unpretentiousness, and gumption. *William Mitten,* in contrast, provides an antithetical portrait of Georgia life—the life of plantation owners, slaveholders, wealthy widows, social climbers, all of whom were out of contact with the pioneer spirit. Longstreet clearly believed in a synthesis of the two ways. As a man of letters, a teacher, and a landowner, he was happy to associate himself with an aristocratic ideal, but he also considered himself a pioneer. As we have seen, his literary attempts to chronicle the mountaineer's South stood in contrast to the plantation literary tradition, the pervading literary force in the Old South, and his university career began as a kind of missionary response, for he hoped to bring culture by establishing discipline and order in unsophisticated, uninformed communities.

William Mitten is a decadent alternative to *Georgia Scenes.* It is the story of people corrupted by affluence, easy living, and superficial cultural superiority. While the sketches were the product of Longstreet's younger days and are full of optimism, *William Mitten* is the product of late middle age. It reflects his personal disappointments and his anxiety over a rapidly changing world.

One surprising aspect of *William Mitten* is that Longstreet preferred to reveal the environmental forces that molded his hero rather than investigate factors of heredity. This provides an incongruous modernity to an otherwise old-fashioned book. As a result of his contact with people in so many different walks of life, Longstreet was an effective observer of human psychology, and he provided his characters with believable actions and reactions to the events they experience.

In an era when a boy's character traits were so often attributed to his inherited "nature," information about that nature is provocatively absent in *William Mitten* since William's father is dead when the novel begins; and the author never reveals what kind of a man he was, how he made his money, or what special qualities his friends remembered about him. Was Mitten senior an unspeakable man, a wastrel, or an excellent, virtuous person? No evidence exists in either direction. Technically the answer for this is that William's father figure in the story is his uncle, Captain Thompson, a thin disguise for Longstreet himself. If Longstreet had cast himself as William's father he might have been responsible in part for the boy's "ruin" which would never have done, and besides, he intended that Mrs. Mitten's neurotic anxiety over her son and her permissiveness be seen largely as the result of her untimely widowhood. The subtitle's emphasis on William's "bad luck" is fundamentally demonstrated by his having lost his natural father.

The reader perceives this stroke of bad luck immediately even though Longstreet at times disregards William's need for a father. The writer focuses on William's mother and shows that he understands people intuitively, presenting her with a fullness perhaps in excess of his intentions. He tells us simply that Mrs. Mitten is a pious, admirable woman, whose "faults lean to virtue's side," but he goes on to create an intriguing, ambiguous character. The average reader will perceive traits in Mrs. Mitten that the author may or may not have intentionally revealed. She is vain, extravagant, and neurotically overanxious and indecisive. Her character may have been based on one of the formidable mothers who had plagued him at Centenary or she may epitomize for the author certain concepts of femininity that concerned him on a less conscious level. She is not the paragon of all earthly virtues that we find among aristocratic Virginians in the plantation novels of Thomas Nelson Page or in George Bagby's stories.

In the first chapter of the novel, Mrs. Mitten is presented as a wealthy widow with a son and two daughters, who are seldom mentioned in the book except toward the end when we learn indirectly that they have made "good" (financially and socially sound) marriages. The focus of the novel is always on William and his relationship with his mother. We are told that he is both mentally precocious and physically beautiful and that his mother vainly parades him before her friends and relatives, thrusting his presence on them at adult gatherings. He becomes not only a momma's boy but a favorite of all the ladies who visit Anna Mitten. Some suggest in a sinister way that the little boy is too perfect to live, that "often it is the case that children with such wonderful gifts die early" (5–6). At eight William is placed in a girls' school (this was not a rarity among upper-class males in this region); after two years, however, his teacher suggests that William is "too pretty and too smart to be in a female school" (6). There is a hint of sarcasm in Longstreet's revelation that Mrs. Mitten took "six months to deliberate what was next to be done with him" (6). A tendency toward indecision in most matters, including her son's upbringing, dogs Mrs. Mitten throughout the book.

That a little boy should read poetry and Biblical passages to crowds of admiring ladies was clearly offensive to the author who prided himself on a rugged masculinity and believed Mrs. Mitten's style of child raising was effete and perilous. Lavish dress always denoted decadence to Longstreet, as it does to his spokesman Captain Thompson, who bitterly derides his sister's elaborate costuming of her son. When William is finally sent to a boys' school, his clothes are so extravagant that his presence in the classroom disrupts it. In this school William meets John Brown, a homely country boy based partly on Longstreet's friend McDuffie, who is unimaginative but virtuous and who is dressed in fragments of bed quilts. Thus Longstreet introduces an important subplot, the success of a poor boy at the expense of a rich boy, with a kind of *Prince and the Pauper* theme. John Brown is neither rich nor good-looking, the antithesis of William, yet it is he who ultimately triumphs in the novel as the better man.

Laughing out loud the first time he sees John Brown's ugly face and shabby clothes, William displays the thoughtless but normal reaction of a little boy who has known only wealthy, beautiful people. John Brown is whipped for his angry response to William's insulting behavior and William's conduct is unjustly ignored by the schoolmaster. It is tempting to conjecture that Longstreet, who identified strongly with McDuffie, saw John Brown as a composite picture of his friend and himself. William, on the other hand, possessed qualities he may have envied or that he imagined his own mother had valued. William succeeds early in school, unlike the author whose memories of the dunce stool were still humiliating. A fatherless boy receives no whippings, has no household chores, and no male competition for his mother's affection. Longstreet had an imposing, implacable father and five brothers and sisters. Young Mitten's ultimate ruin, then, may be a fantasied vindication for slow, graceless, little Gus Longstreet's harassing early years. In contrast to the author's boyhood, William's seems free from academic frustrations, but his easy success leads him to put off his assignments till the last minute or to forget them altogether. Caught unprepared, he lies to his teacher, and when his deceit is discovered he is at first forgiven, but additional uncompleted assignments and subsequent lies result in his being punished at school. In his shame he conceals his beating from his mother and appears to be contrite. At this point, the notorious gossip, Mrs. Glib, confronts Mrs. Mitten with the story of William's beating, and the boy's mother in indignation withdraws him from the school. Mrs. Glib is a horror of an emotional, irresponsible female and an unusual figure in southern literature at this time.

The picture of Mrs. Glib and Mrs. Mitten searching William's white legs for possible traces of whiplash, alternately exclaiming "Oh, my poor, blessed, little innocent angel-lamb" (12), has a high comic quality and also a note of pathos. For the two women force William into still another lie—to deny that he had hidden his textbook to avoid studying it. Longstreet reveals some genuine insight into the young boy's psychology when he shows how a basic impulse toward an honest confession is thwarted by a mother's hysterical denial of his guilt. There is the suggestion that William is virtually forced to prevaricate. Anna Mitten's maternal pride in her son's natural abilities and in his presumed innocence leads her to remove William from Mr. Markham's school despite overwhelming evidence of the boy's duplicity. Even when she later realizes her mistake, she is unable to apologize to Markham or even to acknowledge her error because she has confused William's honor with her own vanity and pride. Out of school William drifts into the company of the shiftless Glib boys and begins to fabricate excuses for his absences from home, announcing to his willfully unsuspecting mother that he is at the Juvenile Debating Society or prayer meetings or lectures. The Glib boys sound like similarly precocious, unsupervised boys anywhere in the country; they lived to climb, run, hunt, play cards, chew tobacco, and drink whiskey. The first clue of their innate depravity is Longstreet's assertion that the boys were "abolitionists of the most generous stamp; disdaining the distinction of colors" (18). The Glibs share some of Huckleberry Finn and Tom Sawyer's qualities, but unlike Twain, Longstreet did not admire free spirits who question the basic assumptions of their society, including racial segregation, and so he depicts them as mindless, amoral, and corrupting.

As a consequence of William's withdrawal from Markham's academy, John Brown becomes the institution's leading scholar. Longstreet may be acknowledging here that his own accomplishments were more a matter of seized opportunities and hard work than of natural ability. Here and at other times in the book, John's self-deprecating remarks about his appearance are intended to convey the boy's modesty, good humor, and adaptability to circumstances, yet neither John nor the author who created him can disguise the hurt beneath his words nor the defensiveness of attempts to turn a natural disadvantage into an asset. Although he is no longer a student at Markham's, William is forced to look on as John Brown triumphantly carries off all the academic prizes on graduation day, but he also watches his oafish rival exalt somewhat masochistically in self-abasement. John begins his class day speech wittily, perhaps, and yet his humor newly dramatizes his self-consciousness: "Ladies and gentlemen: You will not be surprised that I should have selected as my theme for your entertainment this afternoon the incidental advantages of *personal beauty*" (19). The reactions of the class day gathering reveal not only the manners of nineteenth-century

Georgia but also suggest the sort of audience that responded
to the Longstreet brand of humor—crude, unsophisticated, honest, but rather insensitive to nuances of human feeling. For example, John Brown's opening witticism is greeted by immoderate
laughter and floor thumping, so that "it seemed that the house
would be knocked to pieces." Irreverent commendations filled
the air: "Well done flat-head! Hurra shortneck! Bravo pug-nose.
I tell you stiff-leg is some! Give me homespun at last (20)."[2]
    Brown's oration is a triumph of sorts, yet it is hard to believe
that William Mitten could envy John his notoriety. Clearly, if
William had stayed at Markham's school, he would have given
a different type of valedictory address—something more sub-
dued, polished, and intellectual, and he would have expected
a more dignified response from his audience. William's jealousy
of John Brown's awards indicates his natural desire to compete
with other boys and is a healthy sign that his energies could
still be channeled into accomplishments that would nurture his
self-esteem. But Mrs. Mitten fails to procure a tutor for the
boy and his only diversions are provided by the Glib boys,
who, being no match for him intellectually or in any other way,
merely increase his sense of purposelessness and guilt. For one
thing, he has to make up excuses or lie in order to see the
Glibs, and when he is accused of misbehaving with them he
has to deny the association as well as the guilty act.
    Mrs. Mitten's groundless faith in her son makes his situation
all the more complex because her affirmations of his innocence
increases his sense of guilt. Longstreet seems to suggest that
Mrs. Mitten's fear of confronting the truth about her son is a
major hindrance to the boy's development. He probably would
have attributed her unrealistic attitudes to a naivete which sprang
from her own innate goodness and simplicity of character, but
a reader would more likely perceive a neurotic refusal to accept
William as he is, a desire to protect her own shaky self-esteem
regardless of the psychic cost to her son. For example, Mrs.
Mitten forces William into denying that he helped the Glib
boys disrupt a church meeting by making noises outside the
building, as harmless as that might seem. And when strange
whistling noises surround the Mittens' home in the evening,
Mrs. Mitten accepts without suspicion William's immediate recollection of the Juvenile Debating Society meetings and grants

him leave to attend them. Similarly when William breaks his arm trying to steal apples with the Glib boys—and the author views this much more as an intentional violation of God's commandments than as a natural youthful enterprise—Mrs. Mitten encourages his story about an "accident" on the way to the debating society.

A pathological syndrome clearly develops wherein William finds it impossible to acknowledge any error in judgment or petty sin to his mother, a situation tacitly encouraged by Mrs. Mitten's desire to have a "perfect" child. Surely, the frantic mother's conviction that her son is "doomed" to ill luck and a life of misery encourages his proclivities toward rebellious behavior and establishes expectations he could easily fulfill. After his broken arm heals, William gets drunk with the Glib boys. His mother, asking the doctor if her son is indeed intoxicated, reveals a secret motive in her permissive attitude. To the doctor's affirmative reply, she shrieks, "Then my fate is sealed. I am doomed to wretchedness for life" (30). Her response suggests more than a classic overreaction to stress; it is almost a martyr's appeal as if Mrs. Mitten is the victim, rather than her son. Did Longstreet see that William was being made a scapegoat to Mrs. Mitten's delusions of wronged motherhood? Perhaps not. Yet Mrs. Mitten's protest seems so blatantly exaggerated and comic, one must wonder if Longstreet is being at least partially ironic.

Perhaps Anna Mitten was molded on one of Longstreet's own sisters or on the wife or widow of a friend. Anna's brother, who seems so clearly to resemble the author and to be a spokesman for his own views, never castigates her, and when provoked by her behavior, he says only that she takes her tenderness and generosity to an extreme. The reader is more inclined to perceive her as silly, affected, and vain. She is easily flattered, and when a Dr. Twattle becomes William's tutor, she falls in love with him immediately and plans to deliver her fortune into his hands. Her brother, who like Longstreet believes he can detect a flawed character on a first meeting, helps uncover Twattle's fraudulent credentials, and the latter runs out of town to escape the law.

Yet Thompson is unable to find fault with his sister directly for her romantic vulnerability. Instead he attacks William, whose need for a tutor has led to a situation he deplores: "You young scoundrel . . . you've brought things to a pretty pass. . . . would you had died at birth" (43)! The captain's shocking declaration attests to his intense anger at his sister's folly, which he sublimates by bullying his nephew, so that the latter is often the recipient of a rage unconsciously intended for the faultless Anna. William eventually enrolls in a local school but soon falls under the influence of mischievous boys. Longstreet speculates that the naive democratic spirit of the young often subjects them to the tyranny of unworthy persons: "School boys make too little distinction between virtue and vice anyhow. . . . Hence the vicious are admitted to all the rights, privileges, and immunities of the little republic, as fully and freely as the most virtuous" (51). In this case, William seems more like the corrupter than the victim, however, since his superior card-playing ability soon bankrupts the student body. When Mrs. Mitten is finally confronted with overwhelming evidence of her son's gambling, she agrees to entrust the boy's education and upbringing to her brother. The captain proposes Dr. Waddel's boarding school in South Carolina for William because he says the boy's character "is rotting here faster than a dead rat in August" (59). Anna Mitten agrees to the captain's decision because her own fierce pride will not allow her to return her son to Dr. Markham's academy. Longstreet, who on numerous occasions withdrew from various institutions, organizations, and gatherings because of wounded pride or resentment, nevertheless recognizes the vanity of such behavior in others.

The lengthy description of Waddel's school is obviously nostalgic, but it provides a clear picture of a superior educational facility in the early nineteenth century. Young males from privileged families were regimented in an austere, almost monastic environment, which contrasted sharply with the opulence of most of their homes. In the tradition of notable English boarding schools, such as Eton, Harrow, or Rugby, students were encouraged to be aggressive but responsible, to practice various forms of self-denial for future gain, to acquire traits of leadership and a "masculine" demeanor. The discipline required to master Greek and Latin made those languages the foundation of the academic curriculum. Besides admiring the pedagogy of Waddel's school, Longstreet affectionately describes every building in town where the school is located. At one point he alludes to his own story, "The Debating Society," when the captain points out James L. Petigru's office to his nephew, noting that Petigru was "not the Mr. Pentigall of *Georgia Scenes*" (68), although he acknowledges that the tale was set in this same town. Longstreet also has a chance to compliment all the social and financial leaders of the South when the captain points out the long list of distinguished men whose sons, nephews, and grandchildren are presently enrolled in the academy. William settles into Waddel's academy with relative ease. He is astonished by the academic prowess of the other boys. The leader of the class is given 1,000 lines of Latin to translate and even the slowest student must do 150 lines. A heavy emphasis is always placed on the quantity of required work and the need for self-discipline. Fascinated, William also watches Dr. Waddel hold court on disciplinary matters. One of his decisions involves Austin B. Overstreet, a bright prankster who has mixed up English with his Greek recitation. One guesses that Longstreet is recalling an episode from his own youth; at any rate Dr. Waddel is amused at Overstreet's ingenuity and pardons him. Ned Brace from *Georgia Scenes* appears as a tease who chases the other boys with a dead cat. Brace later taunts William for his too feminine appearance, but the author seems sympathetic to Brace's cruel jokes and scornful of William's discomfort.

When the captain returns from South Carolina, he is more interested in discussing the famous people connected with Waddel's school than William's adjustment to it. While the affectations of some people in society may distress Captain Thompson, he seems to be easily impressed by families of wealth and power and is a prodigious name dropper as well.

William's start at Waddel's appears propitious since the headmaster himself tells Mrs. Mitten that William is "destined to a most brilliant future" and that he is a "moral, orderly, studious" person (87). Her reaction is curious: "Brother," she complains to the captain, "I am just as happy as any mother can be at such tidings; but what do they signify, when my poor child may be brought home to me in less than a month, a corpse?" (88). Her solicitude borders on the ridiculous, and even the captain suggests her unrealistic attitudes toward William may be his greatest misfortune.

In the middle of the novel, Longstreet writes a digressive

chapter on the captain's formula for a happy marriage, material probably drawn from the Longstreets' marriage. The captain is a stern disciplinarian but his wife accepts his authority, especially his theories about raising boys. The Longstreets had no sons who lived to the age of William Mitten, but they did share the guardianship of their nephew James after his father's death. Like William, James Longstreet was physically attractive and voted the handsomest cadet at West Point. Possibly his uncle tried to justify his own sternness in his portrait of Captain Thompson. Mrs. Thompson, perhaps using the words of Mrs. Longstreet on some occasion, defends her husband's hard treatment of William: "I reckon it is a wise arrangement of Providence, that men shall not have much care and sympathy, that is as much as we [women] have—that they may not be led off by their affections into too much indulgence" (91). Here as elsewhere in Longstreet's writings women pose a continued threat to self-denial, discipline, and physical courage, which the author sees as essentially "masculine" traits. In the ideal household, the father rules in all matters of importance though the wife's minor idiosyncrasies may be indulged. Speaking of the Thompsons—and perhaps himself and his wife, Longstreet observes: "Whenever a material issue occurred between the heads of the family, his [Thompson's] judgment was final and conclusive; but in matters of minor importance both acted independently" (93). Despite the obvious definition of sex roles, the Thompson's marriage appears to have been a mutually satisfying, productive relationship. So much of Longstreet's writing satirized improper behavior, it is interesting to glimpse what he considered a successful formula for living.

Longstreet follows this picture of domestic contentment with two chapters that attempt to prove, primarily, the foolishness of mothers and, secondarily, the unreliability of Negroes. Anna Mitten, convinced that William is starving, orders her servant Tom to take rich, unhealthy food, lavish clothing, and expensive bed linens and blankets to William at the academy. Unable to recall the name of the school or the directions Mrs. Mitten has given him, Tom becomes hopelessly lost and Captain Thompson is greatly inconvenienced by having to rescue him. The author is in obvious agreement with Thompson's low opinion of the Negro mentality, and Mrs. Mitten's disapproval of her brother's tendency to "underrate the negro character" (113) is seen as another example of her poor judgment. Even Tom's dialogue is made to reinforce Longstreet's viewpoint, for he says "If I had forty thousand niggers, I'd never sen' one so far from home by he'self" (121). The captain's anger at Tom leads curiously to a religious conversion. Criticized by a farmer for his use of profanity in the presence of the Negro, Thompson goes through a period of intense introspection which results in his embracing the Methodist faith. Yet, it is not his immoderate anger at Tom, but his improper use of the Lord's name that causes regret and leads him to repent. Perhaps Longstreet was unable to write about the personal tragedy, the loss of his little boy, which resulted in his own conversion. The captain's more superficial reasons for religious affirmation may have allowed the author's still painful memories of little Alfred to remain suppressed.

At this point the novel's focus divides as the captain's growing religious awareness leads to numerous digressions. In one chapter, Mrs. Glib converts to Methodism on her deathbed, thereby saving her own soul, one assumes, but too late to alter the wretched fates of her children. An indulgent widow, she has failed to inculcate proper values in her children who face ruin and disgrace after her death. In addition, Longstreet devotes an entire chapter to a discussion between the captain and Mrs. Mitten on the subject of religious denominations. Anna remains a Presbyterian but becomes more tolerant of Methodism's "cruder" rituals: "Verily, brother, you have said more in defense of shouting than I supposed could be said; and most untruly; if I never shout myself I shall always, hereafter, look with the greatest indulgence upon those Christians who do" (144). Was the author here recalling some of his dignified wife's early qualms about the Methodist congregation?

Meanwhile, William's fortunes turn and he becomes the leading student at Waddel's, admired by faculty and boys alike. The captain is so pleased he gives the boy a horse named Snapdragon. Considering that he later quotes Doctor Waddel as saying "show me a school boy with a horse, dog, and gun and I'll show you a boy who will never come to anything" (164), Thompson's gift seems rather perverse. Is he deliberately tempting William? After such a brief period of success and high self-esteem, William with the unwitting aid of his horse begins a slow but steady decline. First, he meets up with rough, hard-drinking companions on his excursions through the countryside during vacation. Back at school he is able to board farther away from Dr. Waddel and thus falls under the pernicious influence of Smith and Jones, two students whom the author offers as proof "of the doctrine of natural depravity" (165). Having purchased whiskey and tobacco for Smith and Jones and playing cards for himself on an excursion with Snapdragon to a nearby town, William is discovered by Dr. Waddel. He admits that he has gambled and melodramatically laments, "I'm disgraced, I'm ruined" (170). William's terrible remorse and his Faustian sense that he has transgressed too far to begin anew are reminiscent of his mother's exaggerated earlier declarations.

Before he can be disciplined, William is called home to his uncle's deathbed. Once more the boy is deprived by fate of a male role model. Furthermore, his pride prevents his returning to school to accept his punishment, paralleling his mother's obstinate refusal to return William to Markham's school several years previously. Markham, interestingly, provides the solution, since he arranges for William to go to Princeton with his own son, George Thompson, and William's old acquaintance, John Brown. According to the narrator-author, "Princeton was, at that time, in the South, at least, the most renowned College in the Union" (180). Longstreet may still have held a special affection for the college located in his mother's birthplace, and if it had not been for the influence of Calhoun in his days at Dr. Waddel's, he would probably have chosen the New Jersey college. But another departure from the author's own life is significant here. George McDuffie, on whom the character of John Brown partially was based, went to South Carolina out of financial necessity. In the novel, Brown's tuition is raised by Mr. Markham, Captain Thompson, and other affluent benefactors. Longstreet seems to have corrected in fiction what he considered unjust in life, or he may have been alluding to arrangements made for his own tuition at Yale long ago. Mr. Markham prepares the boys for their voyage and their stay at Princeton with a chapter-length sermon; in the spirit and manner of Polonius, he urges them to respect their elders, to avoid profane swearing, and to follow school rules diligently. He concludes by entreating them to burn these seven words in their memory: "Let cards alone, let intoxicating liquors alone" (199). The boys sail from Savannah to New York on the first part of their journey, a detail in the novel that accentuates the expense and difficulty involved in going North to school in the early nineteenth century.

During his freshman year, William meets an attractive, well-bred girl named Louisa Watson. She admires his veneer of refinement and his good looks and, perhaps, perceives that he has a tender, misunderstood nature. When William discovers that Louisa is an heiress, however, his "love" for her is soon underscored by self-interest and he pursues her for the sake of her fortune. At the same time he enters into a secret engagement with Amanda Ward, a girl whose shallow values seem more compatible with his own. The double courtship becomes expensive and soon William begins to spend money wildly and to go into debt. In contrast, John Brown is so frugal that he is able to send money home to his ailing mother (with his benefactors' permission, of course). John is therefore unable to lend money to William and is scorned by the Georgia contingent as a disloyal friend. When the boys discover where Brown has sent his extra money, however, William is the first of them to apologize. This suggests a certain sensitivity and graciousness which makes William a likable and complex character, yet the author seldom draws attention to his better qualities. When such qualities rise to the surface, they never receive the author's clear acknowledgement or approval. Soon, however, William resorts to his old gambling ways to clear up debts. Discovered, he is called before the faculty, where he arrogantly attacks the character of his accuser and boldly denies his obvious guilt. The scene is quite unconvincing because prior to this William has been presented as such a passive person, buffeted by fortune, led into sin by more corrupt spirits. More believable is his grief on returning home to his mother's deathbed where he is urged by her doctor to lie about his dismissal from college, and laments, "Another lie. How sin begets sin" (224).

After his mother dies, William receives a letter from Louisa breaking off their relationship. She could forgive his gambling and dismissal from college, she says, but not his secret engagement to Amanda Ward. Without the prospect of an advantageous marriage, William renews his associations with the local reprobates. An opportunity for a new relationship with Flora Summers is challenged by John Brown's interest in the same girl. Unexpectedly, Flora chooses John despite his lack of grace and physical beauty, saying, "John, it is hard to part with you, you pleasant ugly dog" (235). Longstreet has therefore fulfilled another fantasy: The steady plain-looking man wins the beautiful girl, while his handsomer rival is exposed as superficial and unreliable. John Brown goes on like McDuffie and Longstreet to become a successful lawyer and judge, a credit to his state, whereas William becomes a full-time gambler and is soon "arrested in his career by that disease common to gamblers, and fatal to all, consumption" (237). Before his death William begs forgiveness of his sins, undergoes a sincere religious conversion, and dies with the words, "Mother, receive thy son" (239).

Critical Response

William Mitten was not well received in the author's lifetime. As Judge Fitzgerald observed in his biography of the author, Longstreet maintained somewhat defensively that his purpose in writing the novel had been moral rather than literary and that he did not expect it to be reviewed in the better periodicals. According to Wade, the book was relatively popular among readers of *Field and Fireside,* where it first appeared in installments.[3] This is not surprising since many charming descriptions and passages appear in the work, and small segments escape the deadening effect of the author's continuous moralizing. Writing at the beginning of this century, Carl Holliday noted the popularity of *William Mitten* though he personally admired it less than *Georgia Scenes.*[4] A year before Longstreet's death, James Wood Davidson wrote disparagingly of the novel in *Living Writers of the South:* "To say that *Master William Mitten* is a failure might mislead those who have no idea how terrible a failure it is. It is the author's Moscow."[5]

It is doubtful that Longstreet ever read Davidson's book. If he had he would have been placated by the critic's overpraising of *Georgia Scenes. William Mitten* has been dismissed as an unimportant novel, moralistic, and lacking the vitality and humor of *Georgia Scenes.* The author's talents were better suited to the tale than to full-length fiction; the authorial intrusion increases in his longer work, and Mitten's "biography" is sometimes painfully contrived. The regional flavor of the *Scenes* is missing since Mitten, though a Georgian, is raised in genteel surroundings, and the author has relied very little on natural description or the idiosyncrasies of mountain people or villagers. The novel reflects a change in the author's milieu as he turned from the life of a circuit court judge to that of a college president.

Yet *William Mitten* is in many ways a superior index of the author's literary potential, a more honest appraisal of life as it was actually lived in Georgia during the nineteenth century, and a warmer, more compassionate book than Longstreet had written previously. *William Mitten* reveals more of the author's personal frustrations and preoccupations than his short stories which permitted greater distance between the narrator and his subject matter. Finally, it is a valuable analysis of nineteenth-century educational methods and an indictment of child-rearing customs in that period, exposing the cruel discrepancies between man's expectations for himself and the possibilities of fulfilling those goals. It also shows how the cultural climate of the South immediately prior to the Civil War seems to have been molded by strong American puritan forces.

In *Georgia Scenes* Longstreet presents himself as a keen observer of human traits, a satirist, an amateur linguist, and always a judge of manners, morals, and values. But there were few chances for him to display one surprising facet of his talent: an intuitive understanding of human psychology. Here in Georgia, years before Freud was born, Longstreet provides us with an extremely perceptive analysis of an only son and his psychologically crippling mother. With care he establishes the early influences and experiences of Mitten's life and portrays the characterological weaknesses that plagued the ill-fated boy. With understanding and, with what is even more unusual for the Judge, a kind of tenderness, he records the destruction of a young ego, picturing William trapped in the war between his ignorant, indulgent mother and a harsh, unforgiving society. Naturally, such a view of William's society is this biographer's, not Longstreet's. As always the defender of the status quo and established authority, Longstreet interprets William's tragedy as the direct consequence of irresponsibility. He upholds educators who abuse their power and narrow-minded, self-righteous citizens who loathe William and torment him with religious fervor. Yet he provides us with the facts of William's personal dilemma—the motivations, complexities, and ironies that involve the reader with the protagonist and create a sympathy that carries us through a sad, misunderstood, and needlessly wasted life.

Considered together, *William Mitten* and the earlier *Georgia Scenes* reveal the author's fixed attitudes and values, as well as the idiosyncrasies and the small inconsistencies of his nature that made him a complex, memorable person. Both works mix humor with a frequently sententious moral bias, creating a tone that is occasionally uneven, though seldom dull. When commenting once on the inappropriate sermonizing that often mars Longstreet's narratives, Davidson conjectured that the Judge believed it was "wholesome for the soul that one should yawn from a sense of duty, always after having laughed heartily."[6] Duty and comedy were in some ways the cornerstones of Longstreet's life; the foundation of his literary mission was to teach and to delight. His public, professional, and personal decisions were always the result of rational deliberation in an idealistic Christian context, but his fundamental impulse to laugh immoderately and irreverently at any unexpected disturbance of order and propriety, like a recalcitrant schoolboy, would never be wholly suppressed.

During his lifetime, Longstreet's popularity as a writer fluctuated, depending on which side of his nature he permitted readers to see. In *Georgia Scenes,* the hearty raconteur, the best of the boys of the Georgia bar, conducted his delighted readers on a tour of a unique pastoral landscape while he extolled the values of a community based on order and charity; at the same time he accepted with amused detachment the frailties of human behavior. *William Mitten,* on the other hand, is dominated by Longstreet the judge and moralist. Some readers, to be sure, took comfort in the author's affirmation of traditional beliefs, but it was a cold, righteous comfort that would never appeal to the majority. While Longstreet's novel is an unexpected source of social history and psychological realism for the modern reader, the author's contemporaries were largely intimidated by his pessimistic views of human nature and his doomsday predictions for the modern South. Although conceived by its author at a time of intense personal conflict and growing political unrest in his country, *William Mitten* is nevertheless not entirely tragic in tone. There are colorful natural descriptions, humorous encounters, and nostalgic allusions to Georgia's past in this story, too, but they are overshadowed by the dark presence of an old man increasingly frustrated by his inability to exercise any permanent control over his surroundings.

Chapter Five

From Southern Folk Humor to Local Color

Twentieth-century evaluations of the *Scenes* have consistently taken for granted Longstreet's role as the discoverer of a new literary terrain and as the innovator of a fresh writing style. Beginning with Samuel Albert Link in 1903, whose *Pioneers of Southern Literature* described the Judge as "first among those who may be characterized as the humorists of *ante bellum* days,"[1] critics have begun their discussions of the Piedmont, Georgia, or humorist schools with an appraisal of the *Scenes*. Three years later, Carl Holliday, noting the position of the poor whites in southern letters, called Longstreet's stories of the crackers, "some of the best descriptions of them ever written."[2]

Longstreet's Contribution

In the 1920s, Parrington declared Longstreet to be the original Georgia realist, but undoubtedly Wade's distinguished biography of the Judge in 1924 provided the first significant scholarly investigation of the Georgia author's accomplishment. In addition to laying the fact of the Judge's life before his readers, Wade also placed him in the context of his own culture and discussed the reverberations of his authorship in the works of his contemporaries and their successors:

> In time, Johnson J. Hooper took up the Longstreet literary tradition with his *Simon Suggs* (1845), Joseph G. Baldwin with his *Flush Times in Alabama and Mississippi* (1853), G. W. Harris with *Sut Lovingood* (1867), John B. Lamar in Georgia with *Polly Peablossom's Wedding* (1851), and *Blacksmith of the Mountain Pass,* admired by Dickens. . . .
> . . . The truth is that the *Scenes* exactly suited the taste of the country.

Clayton knew the taste and so did Crockett when together they got up Crockett's *Life.* Minor imitators without number have faded into non-existence: "Jo of Mississippi," who wrote for the *Southern Literary Messenger* in 1845, Abraham Goosequill, Esq., who wrote "The Coon Hunt" for the *Southern Literary Gazette* (Athens) in 1845, and "Ned Brace," who in 1852 favored the *Georgia University Magazine* with four sketches which the student editors characterized as none too good: " 'The Serenade' and 'Turkey Supper,' they pronounce, are passable, but the 'Possum Hunt' is not so good, and the 'Pistol Scrape' is outrageous." *Mississippi Scenes* was an item to be considered by anyone in 1860 who was interested in Mississippi literature, and before the sixties Richard Malcolm Johnston had begun in Georgia the work soon to be published as Philemon Perch's *Georgia Sketches.*

After the Civil War Johnston, Joel Chandler Harris, and many other persons of less note, all of them conscious of their indebtedness to Longstreet, kept alive what he had inaugurated.[3]

During the following decade, Arthur Palmer Hudson credited Longstreet and his imitators with having the wit to realize that something old in talking might look new in writing. That is, he was the first to put the oral tradition of storytelling in print. Edd Winfield Parks described the author as "the first and in some respects the most notable . . . [of those writers who] dealt humorously but realistically with the backwoods Georgia Life."[4] During the 1940s, Clement Eaton and Charles Sydnor acknowledged both the importance of the early Georgia school of writers and Longstreet's crucial role in its initial stages. Eaton called Longstreet "the founder of the school of Southern humorists" and pointed out that "a similar vein was exploited by" William Tappan Thompson, J. J. Hooper, and G. W. Harris.[5] Sydnor also placed Longstreet at the beginning of a long line of regional writers:

William Tappan Thompson, who had been associated with Longstreet in issuing the *States Rights Sentinel,* was the first to follow in the freshly blazed literary trail. In 1840 Thompson published *Major Jones's Courtship,* and he subsequently wrote two more books about the Major. Johnson Jones Hooper of Alabama, who was also a newspaperman, put strong doses of humor and local color into *Some Adventures of Captain Simon Suggs, Late of Tallapoosa Volunteers* (1846) and into the *Widow Rugby's Husband* (1851). . . . Joseph B. Cobb published his *Mississippi Scenes; or Sketches of Southern and Western Life and Adventure,*

Humorous, Satirical, and Descriptive. Two years later Joseph G. Baldwin produced *The Flush Times of Alabama and Mississippi . . .* [in the same tradition].[6]

It may be useful to comment here on other frontier humorists, some of whom Wade and later critics have viewed as Longstreet's major successors. To begin with, Ohio-born William Tappan Thompson (1812–82) was not only a reader of *Georgia Scenes* but, after moving to Georgia in his late twenties, became a personal friend and one-time colleague of the Judge, when the two worked together in 1840 on the *Augusta Mirror.* In that same year, he first praised *Georgia Scenes* in the *Southern Literary Messenger* for its "beauty, sentiment and eloquence of style,"[7] and when his own book, *Major Jones's Courtship,* was published, also in 1840, it contained a flattering reference to Judge Longstreet. Thompson's novel was also influenced by Maine writer Seba Smith's "Major Jack Downing" letters, for he chose her epistolary style over the sketchbook structure of the Addison-Irving-Longstreet tradition. Thompson's major is a slaveholding small farmer with Whig political views, who, with Longstreet, shares a dislike of pretension, heavy drinking, and the pitfalls of urban life.

Five years after the publication of *Major Jones's Courtship,* Johnson J. Hooper (1815–62) wrote *Simon Suggs,* a novel that draws on backcountry folk rather than the beau monde of the plantation tradition. Although Hooper was born in North Carolina, he studied law in Alabama, met his wife there, and stayed on to become the state's most famous nineteenth-century author. In *Simon Suggs,* he presents a spectrum of rural life through the eyes of his roguish hero, Simon. The book is more unified than *Georgia Scenes* because of Hooper's emphasis on a single character, and it lacks the continual moralizing of the earlier work. Hooper's minor characters strongly resemble Longstreet's, however, and he acknowledged in a later work, *The Widow Rugby's Husband* (1851), that his own dirt-eating Young Coats is so similar to Ransy Sniffle that he "might as well pass for that worthy's twin brother."[8]

Another Georgia writer influenced by Longstreet's techniques was "Bill Arp" or Charles Henry Smith (1826–1903), who began writing the "Bill Arp" letters in 1861. The letters were usually addressed to famous people and satirized major political issues. In *Bill Arp, So Called* (1866), the author recounts some adventures that are reminiscent of "The Fight" and "The Gander-Pulling" in *Georgia Scenes*. After the war, two other well-known writers emerged whose style and subject matter acknowledged a debt to the Judge's stories. Richard Malcolm Johnston (1822–98) and, especially, Joel Chandler Harris (1848–1908) were two of the most significant southern writers in the last quarter of the century. Johnston, a middle Georgian who, like Longstreet, was a deeply religious man, becoming first a Baptist preacher and then a convert to Roman Catholicism, wrote humorous sketches in the manner of *Georgia Scenes*. In fact, as his recent biographer has pointed out, Johnston's publication in 1864 of *Georgia Sketches* indicates that his writing was "obviously and even opportunistically in the tradition of A. B. Longstreet's famous *Georgia Scenes.*"⁹ Merrill Skaggs has also pointed out analogies between Longstreet's "The Fight" and Johnston's "King William and His Armies." But it was *Dukesborough Tales* (1871), composed of similar sketches of Georgia life, that brought fame to its author and earned him a reputation for a genial, rambling charm. Harris, a friend of Johnston's, was also an intimate of Longstreet's friend, Thompson, since the two had once worked together on the *Savannah News*. Wade has speculated that Hooper thereby provided a link between Longstreet and Harris and a possible source of anecdotes about the Judge.¹⁰ In any event, Harris in 1893 noted the importance of Longstreet along with Hooper, Thompson, and Johnston in the literary history of middle Georgia.¹¹ Harris is best known for his analysis of plantation life in *Uncle Remus: His Songs and His Sayings* (1880), for his skill with reproducing Negro dialect, and for his awareness of the painful complexities of black-white relations; but he is also a superb storyteller in the old middle Georgia tradition.

In 1954 Jay Hubbell's monumental history of southern writing, *The South in American Literature, 1607–1900*, was published, and three years later, Bruce McElderry brought out a new edition of *Georgia Scenes*. These works contributed to a revival of interest in Longstreet since Hubbell succinctly summarized the Judge's career, surveying recent scholarship on *Georgia Scenes* and emphasizing its author's prominent position among southern humorists, and since McElderry again proved that a nineteenth-century Georgian might still offer valuable insights into life in the Piedmont South. More recently, Louis Rubin has connected Mark Twain with the tradition pioneered by Longstreet, a suggestion offered earlier by Parrington. Rubin discusses the tradition that began in "Longstreet's rural Georgia" and moved westward, a "subliterary, journalistic tradition . . . based squarely on the humor implicit in the confrontation of gentlemanly refinement and breeding with the vernacular shrewdness and realism of the new country beyond the Appalachians."[12] Bert Hitchcock, speaking even more specifically of the literary heritage of humorists who successively influenced new generations of middle Georgia authors, claims "the diadem, as it were, passed from the founder of the line, Augustus Baldwin Longstreet" to Thompson, "Bill Arp," Johnston, Harris, and Harry Stillwell Edwards (1855–1939).[13] To the list of writers inspired by Longstreet, Holman has most recently noted Erskine Caldwell, whose "decayed creatures," he suggests, are "drawn with the humor and detached anger that was in *Georgia Scenes.*"[14]

The Judge's view of the poor whites in his region has been the subject of some controversy. As already noted, Cook believes dirt-eating Ransy Sniffle and other grotesques in *Georgia Scenes* betray the author's basic insensitivity to the genuine problems of the frontier's rural poor. On the other hand, Skaggs has argued that Sniffle serves to contrast with more upstanding rural types in the *Scenes.* She insists that "the farmer [in Longstreet's works] appears preferable in every way to his wealthier and more educated contemporary in the city," and she later commends his "respect for plain folk."[15] While Cook is certainly correct in noting the Judge's condescension, Skaggs' recognition of the agrarian ideal expressed in many of the *Scenes* is, perhaps, more significant. Longstreet did respect the plain people of Georgia's beginnings, but he also saw specific advantages in education, organized religion, and cultural refinements, when not carried to excess. At least in his youth he believed the pioneer or poor farmer had the potential to become an ideal citizen, given sufficient opportunity. Later, Cook's assessment of the author's growing impatience with disadvantaged people seems valid, particularly by the time he was writing such stories as "Darby Anvil" with a distinct bias of antipopulism.

The Reputation of *Georgia Scenes*

Critics in the past century and a half have consistently and justly called *Georgia Scenes* Longstreet's most important book. Nearly every scholar of southern literature has noted the rich source of materials these sketches of life in middle Georgia provide. The author's style contains an element of surprise in his capturing the speech patterns of native Georgians; his themes, based on regional customs and rituals, offer patterns familiar to human experience but new as fictional subject matter. Longstreet as a trailblazer, the father of pioneer humor sketchbooks, is an established phenomenon.

There are two other facets of his best known work, however, that offer areas for further attention and investigation, which this present study has attempted to explore. First, his complex use of dual narrators in the *Scenes* should be noted. Hall and Baldwin represent twin aspects of the author which he can accept, the country squire and the cultivated judge, but what of Timothy Crabshaw, the mysterious interloper? And what of the intrusion of Longstreet himself and some pointedly autobiographical material, which is introduced into the sketches? And how much of the author is hidden in the multisided character of Ned Brace? Furthermore, *Georgia Scenes* needs to be looked at more closely from the perspective of folklore.

Louis Rubin's recent book, *William Emerson Shoots a Bear: Essays on the Southern Literary Imagination,* presents a sustained discussion of the southern storytelling tradition, particularly the swapping of anecdotes among friends at holiday gatherings or on other social occasions. Even among extremely sophisticated contemporary southerners—French professors, Rhodes scholars, and the like—Rubin notes that the anecdotal tradition continues to survive; it is an integral part of the southern heritage.[16] Like others in his region, Longstreet was well practiced in the narrative arts, always prepared for an easy exchange of jokes and tall tales that would make family occasions and visits more memorable. In all likelihood he had his match in any county in Georgia and in many different levels of society, for the oral tradition, unlike written literature, is hostile to class boundaries. He was fortunate to have a wider perspective on what he saw than many other storytellers because of his obvious educational advantages and his experiences traveling as a circuit judge. But what set him above his counterparts in nearly every other Georgia household was his decision to write down what he heard and what he had been telling for years. He did it casually, unaffectedly, and in haste. Parrington has complained about Longstreet's technical sloppiness as have his biographers, Fitzgerald and Wade, but his strength as an author lay in his very lack of concern for literary perfection, and surely his best stories are not "literary." Rather, they are warm, racy, sly, folkloristic studies in human behavior, as well as affectionate appreciations of the natural beauty Georgians could find in their mountains and forests.

As a writer, Longstreet would have been too prideful to listen while an editor pointed out the flaws in his narrative constructions or complained about unfinished characterizations of his minor figures or decried his non sequiturs and plot contradictions. He was always implacably resistant to advice on any issue, following his own guidelines in manners and morals; in this instance, his maddening stubbornness was beneficial since the spontaneity and naturalness of the tales might have been lost had their author been a perfectionist in matters of style or even simply a conscientious student of good writing. Whenever he lost the voice of the storyteller in *Georgia Scenes,* he unfortunately became a preacher.

Very likely this faltering in his narrative seldom, perhaps never, occurred when he recounted the stories in person. The ineffectiveness of his later writing can largely be attributed to his growing self-awareness in relation to the impact of the printed page. He recognized that pronouncements on serious issues were gauche and out of place in social settings, such as a holiday luncheon or a dinner party, where he surely would not have embarrassed his wife by haranguing his guests on declining morals in the state of Georgia. But when he was reminded that his words could influence strangers miles—and years—away from his own place and time, he tended to assume his most clerical manner and delivered a jeremiad. It is interesting to speculate that in addition to losing interest in writing as he did in all new projects soon after he had undertaken them, Longstreet had the opportunity to write only one successful book because after he had seen what he had written in print, bound in a single volume, he could never again tell his stories in the old way, the "come to our house and we'll swap some stories" manner of his early life.

Despite the popularity of *Georgia Scenes* in the first half of the nineteenth century, the Judge's literary accomplishments were eclipsed by the dramatic historical events of the 1850s and 1860s. Within a decade after the author's death, however, a new southern literary movement flowered. Sponsored by newly important family magazines, such as *Scribner's,* and stimulated by the spirit of reconciliation that swept through the Union in the aftermath of the war, the local color writers emerged as a significant literary force.

The Local Color Movement

During the last quarter of the nineteenth century in particular, more than a third of the literary output in journals—in some years it may have run as high as two-thirds—was the local color story and its immediate successor, the sentimental romance. Although major writers such as Howells, James, Crane, and Dreiser were experimenting with realism and naturalism and while certain serious writers, such as Mark Twain, had used local color as a stepping stone to realism, the majority of writers, readers, and publishers favored tales that blended regional curiosities with comforting assumptions about the quality of American life. In addition, journal editors began to play a prodigious role in shaping the nation's literary output.

The rapidly increasing market for family magazines reflected certain technological and social changes and was welcomed by aspiring young editors as well as writers. Advances in printing and in the reproduction of illustrations by using halftones made it possible to assemble attractive journals at a modest cost. Publishers and congressmen had worked together to reduce the postal rates for second-class mail from three cents per pound in 1874 to two cents in 1879, and finally to one cent in 1885. Within a burgeoning capitalistic system, businesses were discovering the possibilities of marketing and advertising in magazines. Certain attitudes also played their role in the public's new interest in magazines. Essentially the popularization of culture continued to broaden the base of an educated reading public that began before the Civil War with the expansion of academies and colleges and the distribution of penny newspapers and inexpensive books. The public library movement and the growth of adult education seminars, such as those at Chautauqua Lake, were equally important. This was the heydey, too, of authors' reading tours. Mark Twain, George W. Cable, Thomas Nelson Page—in fact, most major writers of the period—supplemented their incomes by reading favorite stories, poems, and essays on the lecture platform.[17] Inexpensive books were made possible by innovations in printing and publishing methods, and mail-order houses like Sears, Roebuck, and Company often were responsible for distributing them. The American cult of self-improvement flourished in this era of Horatio Alger and the robber barons, and the public was ready for the thinly disguised history and geography lessons upon which early local color sketches and stories were based. People were reading to be educated; they measured in part the literary merit of a work by the information it provided.

Within the local color movement, there were dramatically opposed philosophies, but these individual philosophies tended to be translated, altered, or absorbed into a bland mixture of platitudes acceptable to purposes of an editorial campaign intended to shape the thinking of the American middle class. The magazine was the proper medium for reaching the masses, and local color was felt to be the literary movement best suited to an audience inexperienced but eager to learn. As early as 1870, Thomas Wentworth Higginson argued the benefits of local color in an article called "Americanism in Literature." Higginson stated that American writers would do well to follow Emerson's example and "make allusions to natural objects" (such as the "humblebee"), and he explained that a writer seeking worldwide recognition ought not to omit everything "occasional and temporary" from his work but "make this local coloring forever classic through the fascination of the dream it tells."[18]

The dominant political and social philosophy of the post–Civil War years was nationalism. The war had forced Americans in all parts of the country to reevaluate their commitment to the Union. The westward movement introduced new experiences and attitudes, impressing upon everyone the variety and heterogeneity of American life. A pride in regional differences was found to be compatible with an overall faith in democracy.

As a literary form, local color fiction represented a gentle initiation into realism. It was a blend of romanticism and realism, distant enough from everyday experience to offer a certain romantic charm, providing a gradual transition to realism which made that movement more accessible to readers. The use of charming provincial dialects lowered reader resistance to nonstandard speech and paved the way for the naturalistic speech patterns of twentieth-century fictional characters; concentration in cultural idiosyncrasies prepared readers to accept the ethnic variety of American experience; and close attention to setting, costumes, and other physical details anticipated the modern obsession with environment.

Every area of America boasted its share of local color writers, but in the South, the local color movement was especially significant. The region had produced so few important men of letters before the Civil War that their appearance in large numbers during the years immediately following was observed with startled interest. The war had stimulated the nation's interest in rediscovering this unique region, and periodicals were surfeited with southern materials. Even northern authors, such as New England's John W. DeForrest who wrote *Miss Ravenel's Conversion from Secession to Loyalty* in 1867, found attractive qualities in antebellum southern life, which many portrayed as romantically as any native might do. To most readers and authors, a southern backdrop was a pleasing embellishment for a romantic tale, for the South's downfall added a touch of pathos that moved sentimental readers.

Only a small number of nineteenth-century readers were ready for realism or naturalism. Perhaps the dichotomy between the general reading public and the educated reading public already had begun. The former appeared to expect—and usually got—conservative attitudes and sentimental events in their fiction. And the popularity and subsequent financial success of a work had a declining relationship to the acclaim it received from professional critics and scholars. The concept of the bestseller had evolved, and the idea of giving the public "what it wanted" resulted in pandering to unsophisticated tastes.

A brief look at the commercially successful fiction from the late 1890s until World War I reveals that romance, especially with a historical setting, was a predominant form and that areas used by local color writers, such as the antebellum South, were still considered an ideal backdrop for tales of chivalry and love. Readers who had been conditioned to formulaic local color fiction could identify with the nostalgic, orderly world of Page's *Red Rock,* best-seller of 1898, or they could revel in the glamorous pseudohistory of Mary Johnston's *To Have and to Hold,* bestseller of 1900. Similarly, drawing on the local color aspects of colonial America, New Hampshire–born Winston Churchill wrote *Richard Carvel* (1899) and then turned to the Civil War scene in *The Crisis* (1901). In Indiana, Booth Tarkington's first and best-selling novel, *The Gentleman from Indiana* (1899), blended romance and local color, while his fellow Hoosiers Maurice Thompson and Charles Major were presenting George Rogers Clark in *Alice of Old Vincennes* (1900) and glamorizing the Middle Ages in *When Knighthood Was in Flower* (1898). Churchill's Civil War novel capitalized on the romantic aspects of the conflict between the states and emphasized the adventurous spirit of the time, much as Page had done. Page's *Gordon Keith* and *John Marvel, Assistant* were published during the first decade of the new century, and they projected in a modern setting the same romantic characters and values of the author's Tidewater fiction. Cable's *The Cavalier,* a best-seller in 1901, dealt directly with the Civil War. Both this novel and the play adapted from it offered the public melodrama in a southern setting. The climactic moment of the play's New York production was actress Julia Marlowe's singing of "The Star-Spangled Banner" to a dying Union soldier. The fact that the play was an enormous success helps us gauge the pervasive acceptance of romantic historical backgrounds in that era.

The fundamental values the majority of local colorists had supported in the years immediately following the war had been respect for authority, a rather static vision of social order, and affirmation of charity, self-sacrifice, and a stoical and emotional acceptance of life's vicissitudes, values affirmed in all of Judge Longstreet's writings. They reflected the complacency and optimism of the white middle class in an era when blacks and immigrants were slowly beginning to assert their own position in American life. The same scheme of values underlay the era of sentimental fiction. There was generally an avoidance of unpleasant sociological analysis in such fiction, and characters tended to develop or mature in these works insofar as they were able to reconcile themselves to their environment without excessive expectations of improving their lot. The gift of romantic love was usually considered sufficient compensation for thwarted personal freedom or ambitions.

From the list above, it is obvious that legends of plantation life were still the most popular southern books, as they had been in Longstreet's time when *Swallow Barn* and *Rob of the Bowl* were first published; but writers like Charles Egbert Craddock (Mary Noailles Murfree) in Tennessee and Johnston and Harris in Georgia carried on the tradition of *Georgia Scenes* in depicting the lives of plain people in the Piedmont region. *Georgia Scenes,* as has been noted, was published three times during the last two decades of the nineteenth century—in 1884 and 1897 in New York, and in 1894 in Atlanta. The importance of the Judge's efforts to mine new literary fields has been conceded, but he has always been considered a precursor for the local color movement. With three collections of his work appearing during the heydey of the movement, he seemed to deserve posthumous recognition as a valid contributor. Perhaps this was one reason why Fitz R. Longstreet, the Judge's nephew, published his volume of Longstreet stories in 1912. The local color movement had run its course, but he may have hoped to please those remaining readers with insatiable appetites for tales of the Old South.

Epilogue: Why Longstreet Is Remembered

Had he not been a writer, the Judge's legal career and active participation in politics would have gained for him the respect of other lawyers and professional people in Georgia; and his impressive record in college administration and ministerial work would have additionally extended his reputation throughout the South. As it turned out, he is not well known as a lawyer although he argued a case before the Supreme Court and became a judge. Nor is he widely recognized as a distinguished educator although he was four times a college president. He is remembered because at forty-five he published a collection of sketches which Walter Blair called "the first and most influential book of Southwestern humor,"[19] and which Parrington claimed "set the style that was followed in a long series of frontier sketches, and established the tradition of frontier humor that flowered at last in Mark Twain."[20] Oddly enough, for a man who sought fame for eighty years, the author virtually brushed aside the importance of *Georgia Scenes,* the one achievement that would bring him enduring recognition. For it was Longstreet the author who gained national recognition unexpectedly and almost effortlessly with a single volume of hastily prepared sketches. The present study has attempted to analyze the contents and literary significance of that volume and has surveyed critical responses to the writer's work during the past century and a half. In any evaluation of Longstreet's legacy, four major contributions to the lasting importance of the author and his best known work, *Georgia Scenes,* prevail: the author's use of the well-established southern oral tradition, his fictional explorations of the Piedmont area and its inhabitants, his perceptive analysis of a culture choosing between agrarian and urban values, and his recognition of the potential appeal of a regional literature that would lead in time to the local color movement.

At the heart of the southerner's sense of fellowship is a love of the oral tale and a respect for a gifted storyteller, since a well-told narrative defines the spirit of a community. Walter Blair attributed much of the success of Longstreet's sketches to the author's penchant for "tale-swapping" and his talent for mimicry: "Since mimicry of speech (particularly for purpose of characterization), humorous depictions of men and beasts, and the development of a story with a point are important in the art of story-telling, it seems fairly reasonable to suggest that what was best in *Georgia Scenes* was at least in part derived from the method of the oral tale."[21] Longstreet made the first significant attempt in writing to capture the energy of materials that had once belonged only to folklore.

Next he focused national attention not only on rural Georgia but on the Piedmont South in general, a segment of the nation unfamiliar to most readers. It is true that he sometimes patronized the crackers or trivialized their desperate needs. Depending on the passages they have selected and their social bias, critics have argued with equal conviction that Longstreet damaged the image of the southern poor in his works or that he was among the first to respect them. The important issue here is that he acknowledged a group of people that others had ignored and that in drawing attention to their lives for whatever reasons he enlarged the literary geography of his region.

In all his works, especially *Georgia Scenes* and *William Mitten,* the author describes, in effect, two Georgias: the old Georgia with its pioneer heritage, nourished by cracked corn and the gumption and bravado of its rural settlers, and the newer Georgia with its prospering towns and cities ensnared by false gods of materialism and cultural affectation. The major narrators of *Georgia Scenes* are specialists in the two Georgias. Hall knows the country folk, laughs at them, scolds them, but respects their solidarity and lack of pretensions. Baldwin is himself drawn into the newer affluent drawing-room society, but he satirizes its vanities and moral emptiness. The author, himself attracted to conflicting aspects of the old and new ways, wisely avoids a single point of view in his first book, tacitly admitting that the synthesis of the two orders is impossible. In his second work, however, he unwisely attempts such a synthesis. While Captain Thompson, his narrator, touts the values of manual labor and self-denial and obedience and his nephew William pursues pleasure and freedom from responsibilities, John Brown combines the practical schooling of a harsh rural background with the intellectual refinements of university education, as Longstreet himself had done, to become the author's ideal southern gentleman. The improbability of such a fruitful blending of values, or at least the unlikelihood that the symbol of such a union could effectively invigorate a society, undermines the credibility of the novel. Furthermore, although Longstreet wrote half a century before regional fiction captured the interest of American readers, his unique blend of realism and romance and of rough-and-tumble humor and frequently pious moralizing anticipated the basic paradigm of the local color story. Finally, his best works shared what Clarence Gohdes has called the basic characteristics of the American humorists: "neat repartee, literary parody, Attic salt and devastating irony."[22]

The author's remarkable achievement was to write a first book when he was in his early forties that, despite its somewhat careless assembly and uneven quality, earned for him a permanent place in American literature as an innovative humorist in style and subject matter and as a social historian as well. In time Longstreet's penetrating sociological and psychological insights in *William Mitten* may also come to be recognized. Meanwhile, he remains a southern writer who described his particular corner of the South with humor, candor, and love and who depicted a value system unique to this region. A close look at his career and writings affords major insights into the moral and political conflicts of a developing nation.

Notes and References

Chapter One

1. Charles S. Sydnor, *The Development of Southern Sectionalism, 1819–1848* (Baton Rouge: Louisiana State University Press, 1966), p. 312.
2. Jay B. Hubbell, *The South in American Literature, 1607–1900* (Durham, N.C.: Duke University Press, 1954), p. 668.
3. Wirt A. Cate, *Lucius Q. C. Lamar* (New York: Russell & Russell, 1935), p. 29.
4. Ibid., p. 27.
5. Duc de la Rochefoucauld-Liancourt, *Voyage dans les Etats-Unis d'Amerique* (Paris, 1799), pp. 147–86, in *The Rambler in Georgia*, ed. Mills Lane (Savannah, 1973), pp. 1–15.
6. Mills Lane, ed., *The Rambler in Georgia* (Savannah, 1973), p. xxii.
7. Thomas P. Abernethy, *The South in the New Nation, 1789–1819* (Baton Rouge: Louisiana State University Press, 1961), p. 146.
8. Augustus Baldwin Longstreet, *Georgia Scenes* (New York: Harper & Brothers, 1840), p. 76; hereafter page references cited in the text.
9. David Crockett, *Narrative of the Life of David Crockett* (Philadelphia, 1834), p. 331.
10. John Donald Wade, *Augustus Baldwin Longstreet* (Athens: University of Georgia Press, 1969), p. 10.
11. Ibid., p. 18.
12. Ibid., p. 7.
13. Augustus Baldwin Longstreet, *Master William Mitten* (Macon, Ga.: J. W. Burke, 1889), p. 109; hereafter page references cited in the text.
14. Oscar P. Fitzgerald, *Judge Longstreet* (Nashville, 1891), p. 21.
15. Wade, *Longstreet*, p. 85.
16. Edward Mayes, *L. Q. C. Lamar* (Nashville: Publishing House of the Methodist Episcopal Church, South, 1887), p. 41.
17. Fitzgerald, *Judge*, p. 45.
18. Ibid., p. 169.
19. W. H. Sparks, *The Memories of Fifty Years* (Philadelphia and Macon, Ga., 1870), p. 482.

20. Unpublished letter, Robert Muldrow Cooper Library, Clemson, S. C.

21. A copy of Bob Short's *Patriotic Effusions* in the Bienecke Rare Book Library at Yale University bears a note identifying the author as W. B. Gilley, a New York printer. Since the poem is replete with references to Tammany Hall and filled with special praise for President Monroe and various New York City landmarks, it seems certainly not to be the work of Longstreet.

22. Wade, *Longstreet,* pp. 366–67.

23. Fitzgerald, *Judge,* pp. 60–61.

24. Ibid., p. 68.

25. Ibid., p. 69.

26. Ibid., p. 70.

27. Wade, *Longstreet,* p. 53.

28. James D. Waddell, *Biographical Sketch of Linton Stephens* (Athens, Ga., 1842), p. 32.

29. Augustus Baldwin Longstreet, *Inaugural Address, Emory* (Atlanta: Library, Emory University, 1955), p. 3.

30. Unpublished document, Emory University archives.

31. Judson Ward, preface to *Inaugural Address, Emory* by Augustus B. Longstreet, p. xiii.

32. Helen D. Longstreet, *Lee and Longstreet at High Tide* (Gainesville, Ga.: published by the author, 1905), p. 98.

33. Glenn Tucker, *Lee and Longstreet at Gettysburg* (New York: Bobbs-Merrill, 1968), pp. 160, 164.

34. Wade, *Longstreet,* p. 270.

35. Unpublished letter, Bond Collection, Dickinson College Library, Carlisle, Pa.

36. Unpublished letter, Robert Muldrow Cooper Library, Clemson, S. C.

37. Mrs. O'Neale's hasty remarriage to Senator John Henry Eaton of Tennessee after the death of her husband in the boarding house where all three had lived for many years caused considerable gossip in Washington. Chief among the purveyors of the scandal was Mrs. John C. Calhoun, one of Washington's leading hostesses. President Jackson, whose own wife had been deeply hurt by gossip at the beginning of their marriage, sympathized with the Eatons and was persuaded by Van Buren to reorganize his cabinet to exclude those who had sided with Mrs. Calhoun against the Eatons.

38. Mayes, *Lamar,* p. 45.

39. Unpublished letter, South Caroliniana Library, Columbia, S. C.

40. Unpublished letter (John McPherson Berrien Collection), Georgia Historical Society, Atlanta, Georgia.

41. Wade, *Longstreet,* pp. 303–4.
42. Royce McCrary, "John MacPherson Berrien and the Know-Nothing Movement in Georgia," *Georgia Historical Quarterly* 61 (Spring 1977):35.
43. Ibid., pp. 37–38.
44. A. B. Longstreet, "Know Nothingism Unveiled" (pamphlet printed by *Congressional Globe,* Natchez, 1855), p. 2.
45. Wade, *Longstreet,* p. 312.
46. *DeBow's Review* 29 (September 1860): 383–84.
47. Wade, *Longstreet,* p. 335.
48. Unpublished letter, South Caroliniana Library, Columbia, S. C.
49. Unpublished letter, South Caroliniana Library, Columbia, S. C.
50. Ibid., p. 324.
51. Unpublished letter, Library of Congress, Washington, D. C.
52. Wade, *Longstreet,* p. 324.
53. Augustus B. Longstreet, *Should South Carolina Begin the War?* quoted in Wade, *Longstreet,* p. 340.
54. Wade, *Longstreet,* p. 344.
55. Tucker, *Lee and Longstreet at Gettysburg,* p. 236. Here and elsewhere Tucker challenges the old view that Longstreet was responsible for the South's defeat at Gettysburg, believing he took the blame for Lee's tactical errors.
56. Wade, *Longstreet,* p. 60.
57. Vernon L. Parrington, *Main Currents of American Thought* (New York, 1927), p. 17.
58. Fitzgerald, *Judge,* p. 88.

Chapter Two

1. C. Hugh Holman, *The Roots of Southern Writing* (Athens, Ga., 1972), p. 76–7.
2. Thomas Nelson Page, "A Virginia Realist," preface to *The Old Virginia Gentleman* by George W. Bagby (New York, 1910), p. x.
3. William Gilmore Simms, *The Wigwam and the Cabin* (New York, 1856), preface, pp. 4–5.
4. E. W. Parks, *William Gilmore Simms as Literary Critic* (Athens: University of Georgia Press, 1961), pp. 101–2.
5. Robert L. Phillips, Jr., "The Novel and the Romance in Middle Georgia Humor and Local Color . . . ," (Ph. D. diss., University of North Carolina at Chapel Hill, 1971), p. 145.
6. Holman, *Roots,* p. 179.
7. Ibid., p. 179.

8. Jennette Tandy, *Crackerbox Philosophers in American Humor and Satire* (New York, 1925), p. 75.

9. M. Thomas Inge, ed., *The Frontier Humorists: Critical Views* (Hamden, Conn., 1975), pp. 87, 88.

10. Ibid., p. 89.

11. James Wood Davidson, *The Living Writers of the South* (New York: Carleton Publishers, 1869), p. 338.

12. Inge, *Humorists*, p. 89.

13. Tandy, *Crackerbox*, p. 76.

14. Vernon Louis Parrington, *The Romantic Revolution in America, 1800–1860* (New York: Harcourt, Brace, 1927), p. 172.

15. Sylvia Jenkins Cook, *From Tobacco Road to Route 66* (Chapel Hill, N. C., 1976), p. 5.

16. George W. Bagby, *The Old Virginia Gentleman* (New York, 1910), p. 20.

17. Inge, *Humorists*, p. 92.

18. Ibid., p. 92.

19. Davidson, *Living Writers*, p. 338.

20. Merrill Maguire Skaggs, *The Folk of Southern Fiction* (Athens, Ga., 1972), p. 315.

Chapter Three

1. Wade, *Longstreet*, p. 154.

2. Ibid., p. 154.

3. Inge, *Humorists*, p. 93.

4. Fitzgerald, *Judge*, pp. 88–89.

5. George M. Hyde, *Bookman* 6 (1897), p. 68.

6. Augustus Baldwin Longstreet, *Stories with a Moral* (Philadelphia, 1912), p. 88; hereafter page references cited in the text.

7. Oxford 1 September 1842. Letter, Lilly Library, Bloomington, Indiana.

Chapter Four

1. Fitzgerald, *Judge*, p. 48.

2. A comparable incident of insulting Georgia humor in the Judge's own life may be relevant here. Over the years he was friendly with Dr. Henry Hull of Athens, Georgia, a physician slightly younger than himself who shared his interests in farming and the Methodist church. In 1847, just two years before the Judge began to write *William Mitten,* Hull named his youngest son Augustus Baldwin after his friend, jokingly telling him he did it "because it is such a humorous baby and because he is so unconscionably ugly" (Wade, *Longstreet,* p. 248).

It would be interesting to know if the Judge still recalled Hull's quip when he dedicated the first bound edition of *William Mitten* to him in 1864.

3. Wade, *Longstreet,* p. 333.
4. Carl Holliday, *A History of Southern Literature* (New York: Neal Publishing Co., 1906), p. 162.
5. Davidson, *Living Writers,* p. 339.
6. Ibid., p. 338.

Chapter Five

1. Samuel Albert Link, *Pioneers of Southern Literature* (Nashville, Tenn.: M. E. Church, South, 1903), p. 471.
2. Holliday, *Southern Literature,* p. 161.
3. Wade, *Longstreet,* pp. 166–67.
4. Parks, *Simms,* p. 218.
5. Clement Eaton, *A History of the Old South* (New York: Macmillan, 1949), p. 512, 513.
6. Sydnor, *Southern Sectionalism,* p. 312.
7. Wade, *Longstreet,* p. 166.
8. Hubbell, *South in American Literature,* p. 674.
9. Bert Hitchcock, *Richard Malcolm Johnston* (Boston, 1978), p. 45.
10. Wade, *Longstreet,* p. 167.
11. Julia Collier Harris, *Joel Chandler Harris* (Boston: Houghton Mifflin, 1918), pp. 316–17.
12. Louis Rubin, *William Elliott Shoots a Bear* (Baton Rouge: Louisiana State University Press, 1975), p. 41.
13. Hitchcock, *Johnston,* p. 135.
14. Holman, *Roots,* p. 12.
15. Skaggs, *Folk,* pp. 28, 31.
16. Rubin, *William Elliott Shoots a Bear,* pp. 150–55.
17. According to a recent article by Allan Gribben, "Mark Twain Reads Longstreet's *Georgia Scenes,*" *Gyascutus,* n.s. 5–6 (1978):103–11. Mark Twain often took a well-marked copy of *Georgia Scenes* to read to audiences on his tour.
18. Thomas Wentworth Higginson, "Americanism in Literature," *Harper's New Monthly Magazine,* November 1870.
19. Walter Blair, quoted in preface to *Georgia Scenes* by Augustus Longstreet (Upper Saddle River, N. J.: Gregg Press, 1969), n.p.
20. Parrington, *Main Currents,* p. 172.
21. Blair, p. 57.
22. Clarence Gohdes, introduction to *Georgia Scenes,* ed. F. M. McElderry (Upper Saddle River, N. J.: Literature House, 1969), n.p.

Selected Bibliography

PRIMARY SOURCES

1. Books

Georgia Scenes, Characters, Incidents &c., in the First Half Century of the Republic. (By a Native Georgian.) Augusta: Sentinel Press, 1835. Subsequent editions: New York: Harper & Brothers, 1840; New York: Harper & Brothers, 1884; Atlanta: Franklin P. P. Co., 1894; New York: Harper & Brothers, 1897; New York: Sagamore Press, 1957; Savannah: Beehive Press, 1975.

Master William Mitten; or, A Youth of Brilliant Talents Who Was Ruined by Bad Luck in *Southern Field and Fireside,* 28 May to Nov. 1859. Subsequent editions: Macon: Burke, Boykin & Co., 1864; Macon: J. W. Burke, 1889.

Fitz R. Longstreet, ed., *Stories with a Moral Humorous and Descriptive.* Philadelphia: John C. Winston, 1912.

Voice from the South: Comprising Letters from Georgia to Massachusetts. Baltimore: Western Continent Press, 1847.

2. Stories and Sketches

"The Ball." *States Rights Sentinel,* March 1834.

"The Character of a Native Georgian." *Southern Recorder,* Milledgeville, 1, 8 January 1834.

"The Charming Creature as a Wife." *States Rights Sentinel,* Augusta, 14 April 1834.

"The Dance." *Southern Recorder,* Milledgeville, 30 October 1839.

"Darby Anvil." *Mirror,* Augusta, 30 October 1839.

"The Debating Society." *States Rights Sentinel,* Augusta, 5 March 1835.

"Dropping to Sleep." *States Rights Sentinel,* Augusta, 26 February 1835.

"Family Government." *Mirror,* Augusta, 1838.

"A Family Picture." *Mirror,* Augusta, 1838.

"The Fight." *Southern Recorder,* Milledgeville, November 1833.

"The Fox Hunt," *States Rights Sentinel,* Augusta, 12 February 1835.

"The Gander-Pulling." *Southern Recorder,* Milledgeville, 15 January 1834.

"Georgia Theatrics." *Southern Recorder,* Milledgeville, 1833.

"The Gnatville Gem." *Magnolia,* Charleston, June 1843.
"The Horse Swap." *Southern Recorder,* Milledgeville, 13 November 1833.
"An Interesting Interview." *Southern Recorder,* Milledgeville, 1834.
"Julia and Clarissa." *Magnolia,* Charleston, September-October 1843.
"Little Ben." *Mirror,* Augusta, Spring 1838.
"The Mother and Her Child." *States Rights Sentinel,* Augusta, 2 June 1834.
"The Old Soldiers." *Magnolia,* Charleston, March 1843.
"A Sage Conversation." *States Rights Sentinel,* Augusta, 17 March 1835.
"The Shooting Match." *States Rights Sentinel,* Augusta, 17 March 1836.
"The Song." *Southern Recorder,* Milledgeville, 6 November 1833.
"The Turf." *Southern Recorder,* Milledgeville, 20 November 1833.
"The Turn Out." *Southern Recorder,* Milledgeville, 11 December 1833.
"The Wax Works." *States Rights Sentinel,* Augusta, 19 February 1835.

3. Essays
"From Out of the Fires." *Nineteenth Century Magazine,* December 1869.
"Inaugural Address, Emory." In *Address at Inauguration of President Longstreet* Edited by Judson C. Ward, Jr. Atlanta: The Library, Emory University, 1955.
"Know Nothingism Unveiled." Pamphlet printed by *Congressional Globe,* Natchez, 1855.
"Letters on the Epistle of Paul to Philemon, or the Connection of Apostolic Christianity with Slavery." Pamphlet printed in Charleston, 1845.
"Old Things Became New, I." *Nineteenth Century Magazine,* January 1870.
"Review of Gov. Perry's Article on John C. Calhoun." *Nineteenth Century Magazine,* January 1870.

SECONDARY SOURCES

Cate, Wirt, A. *Lucius Q. C. Lamar.* Chapel Hill: University of North Carolina Press, 1935. Longstreet is seen as a model for young Lamar, who later became the author's son-in-law.
Cook, Sylvia Jenkins. *From Tobacco Road to Route 66: The Southern Poor White in Fiction.* Chapel Hill: University of North Carolina Press, 1976. Cook finds Longstreet generally unsympathetic toward Georgia poor whites and believes his portraits of comic

grotesques in Georgia contributed to cultural stereotyping. The book provides an excellent history of literary attitudes toward a deprived class of southerners.

Fitzgerald, Oscar P. *Judge Longstreet.* Nashville: Methodist Church, South, 1891. This is the first biography of Longstreet. Fitzgerald was a friend of the author and many of those who knew or worked with him. He accumulated all the known facts of Longstreet's life, making his research the basis for all subsequent studies, including Wade's biography. Fitzgerald's attitude toward the antebellum South is unashamedly admiring, and his portrait of Longstreet overemphasizes the old Georgian's piety and selflessness.

Ford, T. W. "Ned Brace of Georgia Scenes." *Southern Folklore Quarterly* 29 (1965):220–27. Ford claims that a circuit court lawyer named Edmund Burke Bacon was the model for Ned Brace in *Georgia Scenes.* Brace, though a Georgian, is comparable to the Yankee trickster figure in folklore, whose urban ways cannot disguise a playful con man.

Hitchcock, Burt. *Richard Malcolm Johnston.* Boston: G. K. Hall, 1978. A well-written, valuable biography of Johnston who was three decades younger than Longstreet but shared a similar background and training. Hitchcock credits Longstreet with being a direct influence on Johnston.

Holman, C. Hugh. *The Roots of Southern Writing: Essays in the Literature of the American South.* Athens: University of Georgia Press, 1972. Holman has collected some of his best known essays in this distinguished volume. Most readers will turn first to specific studies of Simms, Wolfe, or Faulkner, but there are also useful passages scattered throughout on the roots of other writers in southern history and literature. Longstreet's importance as a voice of the Piedmont South is discussed.

Hubbell, Jay B. *The South in American Literature 1607–1900.* Durham, N. C.: Duke University Press, 1954, pp. 666–69, 947–48. In this vast survey of southern writers, Hubbell draws largely on Wade's biography to present an effective summary of Longstreet's life and writings.

Inge, M. Thomas, ed. Introduction to *Augustus Baldwin Longstreet* by John Donald Wade. Athens: University of Georgia Press, 1969. Primarily an evaluation of John Donald Wade's scholarly career. Inge's introduction stresses Wade's belief that Longstreet's life in some ways epitomized the growth of culture in the nineteenth-century South.

_____. *The Frontier Humorists: Critical Views.* Hamden, Conn.: Archon Books, 1975. Inge has collected a series of essays on frontier humorists, including Longstreet, Thompson, Harris, Baldwin, Clemens, and others. The essays on Longstreet include Poe's famous review of *Georgia Scenes* and an early sketch of Longstreet by John Donald Wade.

Lane, Mills, ed. *The Rambler in Georgia.* Savannah: Beehive Press, 1973. An interesting collection of travelogues on antebellum Georgia, valuable as a backdrop for Longstreet's fictional world.

Lynn, Kenneth S. *Mark Twain and Southwestern Humor.* Boston: Little, Brown, 1959, pp. 61–72. Longstreet's possible influence on Twain and analogies between his short stories and Twain's are discussed.

McElderry, B. R., Jr. Introduction to *Georgia Scenes.* New York: Sagamore Press, 1957, pp. v–x (Sagamore Press edition cited in headnote). An evaluation of Longstreet as a precursor to the local colorists, stressing his importance in America's literary history.

McIlwaine, Shields. *The Southern Poor-White.* Norman: University of Oklahoma Press, 1939, pp. 49–51, 57–59. See also pp. 60, 62–63. An early commentary on Longstreet's comic stereotyping of the poor.

Meine, Franklin J. Introduction to *Tall Tales of the Southwest 1830–1860.* New York: A. A. Knopf, 1930, pp. xvii–xix. See also pp. 103, 137, 303, 335, 397, 453, 455–56. Longstreet's influence on regional writers is noted.

Paine, Gregory. "Augustus Baldwin Longstreet." In *Southern Prose Writers.* New York: American Book Company, 1947, pp. 121–22. See also pp. cxxxvii–cxxxviii, lxxv, and 125–33. Selections from out-of-print novel *Master William Mitten.*

Parrington, Vernon Louis. "Augustus Longstreet." In *Main Currents of American Thought.* New York: Harcourt, Brace, 1927, 2:166–72. Parrington admires Longstreet's portrayal of humorous characters as the product of a certain kind of environment. He likes the earthy humor of the stories and tends to ignore Longstreet's occasionally patronizing treatment of his literary subjects.

Poe, Edgar Allan. "Georgia Scenes." *Southern Literary Messenger* 2 (1836): 287–92. Poe's review of *Georgia Scenes* praises its author as a new southern voice. He particularly applauds the author's ability to create an authentic atmosphere and compares Longstreet's written caricatures to Hogarth's paintings. Although he refers to Longstreet's genuine wit, he prefers the slapstick of "The Gander-Pulling" to the subtler "character of a native Georgian."

Sanger, Donald B. *James Longstreet.* Baton Rouge: Louisiana State University Press, 1952. Reference is made to Longstreet's role in educating James Longstreet.

Silverman, Kenneth. "Longstreet's 'The Gander Pulling.'" *Atlantic*

Quarterly 18 (1966):548–49. Silverman claims that "The Gander-Pulling" is symbolic of the divisive effect of the Know-Nothing party on Southern politics.

Skaggs, Merrill Maguire. *The Folk of Southern Fiction.* Athens: University of Georgia Press, 1972. Skaggs has written an extremely perceptive study of various classes of southerners who appear in fiction, noting Longstreet's interest in the rural poor white.

Tandy, Jennette. *Crackerbox Philosophers in American Humor and Satire.* New York: Columbia University Press, 1925, pp. 74–77. A brief but interesting assessment of Longstreet's career and comic talent.

Wade, John Donald. *Augustus Baldwin Longstreet: A Study of the Developments of Culture in the South.* New York: Macmillan, 1924. Wade's book is a fair-minded and comprehensive study of Longstreet's life. Most of his information is necessarily drawn from Fitzgerald's earlier biography since Longstreet's records were destroyed by fire. The Judge is portrayed as an intelligent, versatile, ambitious, and rather headstrong man. Much of the value of the book derives from Wade's insights into the political and social environment of America in the nineteenth century. The character of Longstreet is convincing but fragmented since there is no attempt to follow events in the author's life sequentially. Many passages in this biography require rereading or checking in the index in order to establish a clear chronology.

————. "Augustus Baldwin Longstreet, a Southern Cultural Type." In *Southern Pioneers in Social Interpretation.* Edited by Howard W. Odum. Chapel Hill: University of North Carolina Press, 1925, pp. 119–40. Wade repeats some of the material that appeared in his book. Here he emphasizes Longstreet's discovery of rural Georgia as a new source of fiction.

————. "Old Books: *Georgia Scenes.*" *Georgia Review* 14 (1960):444–47. Wade provides an affectionate reappraisal of Longstreet's major work.

Index